How to Vote with Passion, Purpose and Power

A Voter's Primer

Anthony N. English

authorHOUSE®

AuthorHouse™
1663 Liberty Drive, Suite 200
Bloomington, IN 47403
www.authorhouse.com
Phone: 1-800-839-8640

First published by AuthorHouse 7/15/2008

ISBN: 978-1-4389-0280-7 (e)
ISBN: 978-1-4389-0279-1 (sc)

Library of Congress Control Number: 2008906311

Printed in the United States of America
Bloomington, Indiana

This book is printed on acid-free paper.

"Government is not reason; it is not eloquence, it is force. Like fire, it is a dangerous servant and a fearful master."

George Washington

ACKNOWLEDGEMENTS

A special thanks to my wife, Marilyn for insightful and critical contributions which helped to clarify this effort and to my daughters Stephanie and Lauren for their positive inputs, perceptive critiques, and keen, meaningful suggestions which clearly have improved this effort. Thanks also, to my son-in-law, John Herrera for his contributions and to my sons, Ryan, Cameron and Anthony for their encouragement.

Contents

CHAPTER ONE
What is Voting All About?

"We in America do not have government by the majority. We have government by the majority who participate."

Theodore Roosevelt

This book is directed to all new voters who find themselves in a position to vote for their government leaders whether or not they are local or national candidates.

You may be a young person, now of voting age. An immigrant to this wonderful country, now qualified to vote by virtue of newly earned citizenship. You may be a person who, although qualified to vote, has never done so because you don't understand the elective process.

America: A system of government considered by many to be the best?

The Republic of the United States of America has been considered by many as the best system of government by the people since its inception. Webster's Unabridged Dictionary describes a republic as: "A state or nation in which the supreme power rests in all the citizens entitled to vote (the electorate) and is exercised by representatives, directly or indirectly, by them and responsible to them."

This system has withstood the test of time for over 200 years and its success has been so clearly evidenced by the masses of immigrants that clamor to become part of this land of opportunity even to this day. Furthermore, very few citizens of this country are unhappy enough to leave permanently for other countries or types of government systems. The main reasons for this are the levels of freedom we enjoy. Freedom to worship in any we way we like without government interference, freedom to be educated in any field, freedom to start or run a business of your choosing, freedom to vote privately and, secretly for the person we feel best able to do the job and the freedom to move about anywhere in the country without interference from the government or anyone else. Whether you be a natural born citizen or a naturalized citizen this is a country to be proud of.

Should you be a new voter you are entering an exciting part of your new relationship with this country in voting for your political leaders. While this book has tried to highlight the failures of many of those elected to high office we need to be very clear. There are many, many politicians in office who wish to be effective, just and moral leaders. Our emphasis in this book is on those who have failed to uphold the trusts we extended to them when we voted them in. One of the purposes of this book is to acquaint you with the potential you have to correct these election failures.

This book is, also, directed to those experienced, established and active voters who may always vote but who have been a part of electing politicians who are not qualified to the office. You may be a voter who simply votes for a candidate or a party because a relative always had. You may simply be a lazy voter who does not take the time to learn about the candidate's record or beliefs. You just don't take the time to understand the issues so place your vote based on someone else's decision. As a result, there is malfeasance, criminal activity, waste, and, abuse beyond belief in our current body of senators and congressmen. You can correct this by standing up for yourself and learning to vote with passion, purpose, and power.

The purpose of this book is to entice you and to encourage you to exercise your voting responsibility, as it is said, *"citizens get the government they deserve."* What this means is that because so few voters go to the election booths to place their votes politicians who have no right to get elected are elected. As a result, those elected, now managing your interests are frequently inept, ill informed, self indulgent, fraudulent, and guilty of kickback schemes. Guilty of sexual exploitation of co-workers interns, theft and any number of acts of malfeasance.

• A former president, William Jefferson Clinton (D), who, after lying to the entire country saying he "did not have sex with that woman," was found to have had a sexual relationship with the young intern working for the government at that time. Not only did he have sex with the young girl but he also performed crude sexual acts on her that would have branded any other man a pervert. While an attempt was made to impeach him it failed due to partisan politics by those we elected who apparently don't consider these kinds of acts wrong. Today, he is a respected former president touring the world making speeches and earning millions of dollars as a result of his infamy. His Vice-President, Al Gore, next in line for the presidency, was alleged a liar. He claimed he 'invented the internet' and, it has been alleged, lied regarding his own sister's death. He also apparently lied about a song he claimed his mother used to sing to him even though it was not written at that time.

• Examples of this is Senator Edward Kennedy (D), still in office even though he ran his car off a bridge at Chappaquidick, Massachusetts resulting in the death of his girlfriend/ aide (while still married). He did not report the incident until the following day. It appeared that no apparent effort was made to save the girl who drowned in the vehicle.

• Still operating as a respected congressman is Representative William Jefferson (D), who was caught in an undercover operation taking a $100,000.00 bribe from an officer of the court. The funds were later found in a freezer at his home.

• Congressman, Mark Foley (R) was emailing explicit sexual messages to government interns and as a result had to resign in disgrace after many years as your government representative.

Transgressions like these highlight the importance of being a selective and knowledgeable voter, a voter who then can raise the bar towards more competent, professional leadership. (Leadership who would have a greater interest in improving the lot of all our citizens instead of just their own.) These transgressions favor no political party. All politicians are, potentially, equally guilty of misusing the trust and the office for which they were elected. Never vote for a particular party because you think they are more moral or more dedicated to the people, because this is simply not true.

Who Can Vote

• In order to be able to vote you must be a citizen of the United States and at least 18 years of age and you must be registered as a voter. Registration forms usually can be found at US Post Offices, County offices, at the various political party offices, as well as on line. Currently, the only state where you are not required to register in order to vote is North Dakota.

• Presidents are elected for a term of four years and may serve up to two terms. Senators are elected for six years and representatives are elected for two years. There are two senators elected from each state and representatives are numbered based on the population levels of the state as determined by the most recent census.

Office	Min Age	Term	Citizenship	Limit
President	35 yrs	4 yrs	Natural Born in USA	Two terms
Senator	30 yrs	6 yrs	Citizen for 9 years	None
Congress	25 yrs	2 yrs	Citizen for 7 years	None

• Voting is the single most important thing the individual citizen can do in deciding who will run your country and what kind of government it will be.

CHAPTER TWO
Does My One Vote Really Count?

"I always consider the settlement of America with reverence and wonder, as the opening of a grand scene and design in providence, for the illumination of the ignorant and the emancipation of the slavish part of mankind all over the earth"

John Adams

Many new voters wonder *"With so many millions of people voting how could my single vote really count?"*

Consider these historical events:

1645:   One vote gave Oliver Cromwell control of England.

1649:   One vote caused Charles 1 of England to be executed.

1776:   One vote gave America the English language instead of German.

1839:   One vote decided the Governor's race in Massachusetts.

1845:   One vote brought Texas into the Union.

1846:   One vote resulted in President Polk's request for a declaration of war against Mexico.

1850:   One vote allowed California to be admitted to the Union.

1867:   One vote ratified the purchase of Alaska.

1868:   One vote saved President Andrew Johnson, who had been impeached, from being removed from office.

1876:   One vote changed France from a Monarchy to a Republic.

1923:   One vote gave Adolph Hitler leadership of the Nazi Party.

1941:   One vote saved the Selective Service just 12 weeks before Pearl Harbor.

1960:   One vote more per precinct would have elected Richard Nixon instead of J.F. Kennedy.

Never, never, underestimate the power of your vote. Each of us needs to understand and appreciate the importance of our one vote towards keeping our Democracy working properly.

In the event you don't vote you will have no position with those who are elected and you will have no voice over the actions of the politician who act against your own interests in how the government is run and how your tax dollars are spent.

CHAPTER THREE
Understanding The Issues

"The whole aim of practical politics is to keep the populace alarmed-and thus clamorous to be led to safety-by menacing it with an endless series of hobgoblins, all of them imaginary."

H. L. Mencken

Now, it is also important that we vote with an understanding of the issues being voted on or the person seeking election. History has proven that many officials were elected who never should have been placed in a position of public trust. Your vote is wasted if you vote because the local newspaper supports a particular candidate or because your parents always vote for a particular party. Your vote is wasted if you vote based on gender, ethnicity, age, or because some celebrity supports a particular candidate. You must be careful not to assume that a certain endorsement means a particular candidate is the right candidate for you. Many times endorsements are made simply because money has been donated to the candidate. Once that person is elected then the endorser comes looking for the special favor he purchased in order to help the candidate get elected. You, as a taxpayer, then get hit with an ever increasing tax liability because some unethical politician got elected and your tax dollars are now being spent on some unneeded boondoggle.

No, in order for your vote to mean anything you must learn all you can about the candidate and the issues so you can make your own intelligent decision based on good information and not political hype or partisan influences.

What are the questions you as a voter should ask yourself?

- Does he have ability and integrity & experience?
- What does this candidate stand for?
- What's his position on war?
- What's his position on abortion?
- What's his position re local issues?
- What's his position regarding line item expenditures?
- How does this candidate differ from his opposition?
- Which issues are important to you?
- Will he serve the people or himself?

CHAPTER FOUR
Who Should You Vote For

"When they call the roll in the Senate the Senators don't know whether to answer "present" or "not guilty."

H. L. Mencken

This is the most difficult question a voter faces. This is because most politicians have one goal in mind: to get elected at any cost. Few, if any, really are in politics because they wish to better your world. They wish only to better their world, and the evidence is pretty clear that this is the case. There are innumerable politicians who came to the table with nothing and, after a few years in office, have become multi-millionaires. A good example of this kind of self indulgence is the late, Lyndon Baines Johnson, former President, from the state of Texas, who was a schoolteacher when he first ran, and then was elected to local office. A few years later he was a multi-millionaire due to his ability to manipulate the system to acquire several very lucrative Federal Communication licenses.

An organization called "The Sunlight Foundation" recently reported on examples of how politicians have become wealthy once in office. Senator Barrack Obama when elected in 2004 was worth $328,442.00. By 2006 he was worth $799,000.00

and his wife made $4.2 million in 2007. A representative, Jim Moran, the former mayor of Alexandria, Virginia was in the hole, a negative $12,000.00, and less than ten years later he had $12,000,000.00 in assets. Senator Hillary Clinton was $6 Million in the hole when elected senator of the state of New York. By 2006 she had a net worth of $30.7 million. Many think these kinds of gains are only made by CEO's and businesses but the facts prove otherwise. Politics leads to big personal gains for many of those elected. Remember this when you vote. Are they running for office to help you or are they running to help themselves?

You can see why some politicians will do or say anything in order to get elected. They lie about their own credits, they lie about their opponents, they distort the truth and will do almost anything in order to get elected so they can feed at the government table and have access to the generous income, perks, and retirement we have allowed them to have. But for many even this is not enough so they extort large sums of money from contractors, lobbyists, and special interest groups.

As a result of their personal desires, they misrepresent the facts and simply lie to discredit their opponents.

This, by the way, is not new in politics. Since our country was formed, those seeking political positions have used abusive and aggressively rude treatment of their opponents in order to discredit them.

Many have thought nothing at all of spreading out and out lies about their opponents.

VOTER BILL OF RIGHTS

• You have the right to cast one ballot if you are a valid registered voter. A valid registered voter means a United States Citizen who is a resident of the community in which he or she lives, at least 18 years of age, not in prison or on parole for conviction of a felony, and who is registered to vote at his or her current residence.

• You have the right to cast a provisional ballot if your name is not listed on the voting rolls.

• You have the right to cast a ballot if you are present and in line at the polling place prior to closing of the polls.

• You have the right to cast a secret ballot free from intimidation.

• You have the right to receive a new ballot if, prior to casting your ballot, you believe you made a mistake. If at any time before you finally cast your ballot, you feel you have made a mistake, you have the right to exchange the spoiled ballot for a new ballot. Vote-by-mail voters may also request and receive a new ballot if they return their spoiled ballot to an election official prior to closing of the polls on Election Day.

• You have the right to receive assistance in casting your ballot, if you are unable to vote without assistance.

• You have the right to return a completed vote-by-mail ballot to any precinct in your county.

• You have the right to election materials in another language, if there are sufficient residents in your precinct to warrant production.

• You have the right to ask questions about the election procedures and observe the election process. You have the right to ask questions of the precinct board and election officials regarding election procedures and to receive an answer or be directed to the appropriate official for an answer. However, if persistent questioning disrupts the execution of their duties, the board or election officials may discontinue responding to questions. You have the right to report any fraudulent activity to a local election official or to the office of your Secretary of State.

CHAPTER FIVE
The Major Political Parties
Republicans, Democrats,
Libertarians & Independents

"Under Democracy one party always devotes its chief energies to trying to prove the other party is unfit to rule and both commonly succeed and both are right."

H. L. Mencken

Now let's take a look at the published concepts of each of the major political parties. You may find this information on each of the party's web-site so we have condensed their basic precepts herein. Each party has its own platform, agenda and governing strategy. A voter may wish to study carefully these party concepts and satisfy themselves to a particular parties positions in concert with their own beliefs and interests before casting a ballot. This information was retrieved from the named political party web site.

These parties are referenced here as they represent by some political analysts as the majority of the registered voters. One firm suggested that in 2004 of the registered voters 41% were Democrats, 39% Republicans and 20% Independents. This doesn't leave any room for "others" so it is clearly a broad brush of information but probably comes close to the real situation as far as registered voters are concerned.

REPUBLICAN PRINCIPLES
(Founded 1854)

"I'm a Republican because...

"I believe the strength of our nation lies with the individual and that each person's dignity, ability and responsibility must be honored."

"I believe in equal rights, equal justice and equal opportunity for all, regardless of race, creed, sex, age or disability."

"I believe in free enterprise and encouraging individual initiative has brought this nation opportunity, economic growth and prosperity."

"I believe government must practice fiscal responsibility and allow people to keep more of the money they earn."

"I believe the proper goal of government is to provide for the people only those critical functions that cannot be performed by individuals or private organizations, and the best government is that which governs least."

"Our vision is simple. We want an America that gives all Americans the chance to live out their dreams and achieve their God-given potential. We want an Amer-

ica that is still the world's strongest force for peace and freedom. And we want an America that is coming together around our enduring values, instead of drifting apart."

"I'm a Republican because...

"I believe the strength of our nation lies with the individual and that each person's dignity, ability and responsibility must be honored."

"I believe in equal rights, equal justice and equal opportunity for all, regardless of race, creed, sex, age or disability."

"I believe in free enterprise and encouraging individual initiative has brought this nation opportunity, economic growth and prosperity."

"I believe government must practice fiscal responsibility and allow people to keep more of the money they earn."

"I believe the proper goal of government is to provide for the people only those critical functions that cannot be performed by."

"I believe the strength of our nation lies with the individual and that each person's dignity, ability and responsibility must be honored."

"I believe in equal rights, equal justice and equal opportunity for all, regardless of race, creed, sex, age or disability."

"I believe in free enterprise and encouraging individual initiative has brought this nation opportunity, economic growth and prosperity."

"I believe government must practice fiscal responsibility and allow people to keep more of the money they earn."

"I believe the proper goal of government is to provide for the people only those critical functions that cannot be performed by individuals or private organizations, and the best government is that which governs least."

"I believe the most effective, responsible and responsive government is government closest to the people."

"I believe Americans value and should preserve our national strength and pride while working to extend peace, freedom and human rights throughout the world."

"Finally, I believe the Republican Party is the best vehicle for translating these ideals into positive and successful principles of government."

The Republican National Committee
310 First Street, Washington DC 20003
www.gop.com

THE DEMOCRATIC PARTY
(Founded 1824)

"Today's Democratic Party is determined to renew America's most basic bargain: Opportunity to every American, and responsibility from every American. And today's Democratic Party is determined to re-awaken the great sense of American community.

"That is what today's Democratic Party offer is: the end of the era of big government and a final rejection of the misguided call to leave our citizens to fend for themselves-and a bold leadership into the future: to meet America's challenges, protect America's values, and fulfill American dreams."

Go to www.democrats.org for more details on their platform and published policies.

Address: The Democratic Party
430 South Capitol Street-SE,
Washington, DC

THE LIBERTARIAN PARTY
(Founded 1971)

Issues & Positions of the Libertarian Party

"As Libertarians, we seek a world of liberty; a world in which all individuals are sovereign over their own lives and no one is forced to sacrifice his or her values for the benefit of others."

"We believe that the respect for individual rights is the essential precondition for a free and prosperous

world, that force and fraud must be banished from human relationships, and that only through freedom can peace and prosperity be realized."

"Consequently, we defend each person's right to engage in any activity that is peaceful and honest, and welcome the diversity that freedom brings. The world we seek to build is one where individuals are free to follow their own dreams in their own ways, without interference from government or authoritarian power."

"Libertarians support maximum liberty in both personal and economic matters. They advocate a much smaller government; one that is limited to protecting individuals from coercion and violence. Libertarians tend to embrace individual responsibility, oppose government bureaucracy and taxes, promote private charity, tolerate diverse life styles, support a free market, and defend civil liberties."

To learn more about the Libertarian Party go to www.lp.org

Address: 2600 Virginia Ave-NW, Ste 200, Washington, DC 2007

INDEPENDENT VOTER

An alternate to being a member of a specific party is to register as an Independent voter. A very large percentage of voters in the USA, approximately 20 to 30%, are registered as Independents. This allows them to vote freely for whichever candidate they prefer without being tied to a specific political party or political belief.

There are many other lesser-supported parties and their web site addresses are listed in the index at the back of this book so you may search out their policies and principles as well. Due to their size they usually have little or no impact on an election but may have positions that you are willing to endorse and support.

The three largest parties listed all have what appears to be wonderful principles and ideals. It would seem that no rational voter could really justify not supporting all of them. The truth is, however, that any party that has been in power has not adhered to their own policies and principals.

In the past, there were two major political parties-the Republicans and the Democrats. The Republicans tended to be politically conservative and the Democrats tended to be liberal in their respective political managements of the country. A newcomer to these is The Libertarian Party.

But first, what do these terms, liberal, conservative and libertarian really mean.

Webster's Unabridged dictionary says thus;

Conservative: tending to oppose change; favoring traditional views and values.

Liberal: Having, expressing or following political views or policies that favor civil democratic reforms, and the use of government power to promote social progress.

Libertarian: One who believes in freedom of action and thought.

Independent: A person not a partisan of any political party; one who votes as he or she wishes without regard to party labels.

Your responsibility is to select the party that fits your political desires and beliefs and then to pursue support of that entity by your vote and perhaps by your financial contribution as well.

An analysis of the political landscape would seem to suggest that, over time, changes, possibly even somewhat subtle, have been shifting the relative positions of the parties. The Republicans appear, to the writer, to have moved more to the "left" or Liberal bias and the Democrats appear to have moved more to their left becoming more socialistic in their pronouncements and direction.

The Republicans used to be fiscal conservatives, the promoters of less government and, the party that encouraged us to stay the course as far as our moral values and political standards are concerned. They professed belief in less government.

The Democrats supported social change by government action and force but with the voters support.

Socialism: "A social system in which the producers possess both political power and the means of producing and distributing goods." This really means the government will decide who gets what and how much they will get.

As a result of this shift left by both Republicans and the Democrats, the Libertarian party has sprung up to fill the resulting gap. Thus the Libertarians are, possibly, the only real Conservatives left in the political arena.

As a potential voter you only need to pay attention to what terms the politicians use to learn their leanings. When you hear "national" anything, (example: national medicine) it is usually a Liberal saying it. Should you hear "less government" it is usually a Conservative or a Libertarian promoting it.

As a voter what does it all mean to you? It usually means how much you are going to spend in the form of taxes. The problem with government and taxes is that the politicians have an insatiable desire for more and more of your hard earned dollars. At the same time, as much as half of the money the government collects from you is wasted and/or unaccounted for.

President Thomas Jefferson said, "I think we have more machinery of government than is necessary, too many parasites living on the labor of the industrious." And that was 200 years ago."

President Ronald Reagan said, *"Government is not the solution to our problem, government is the problem."*

These perceptive presidents recognized that government becomes a refuge for the bureaucrat, the hanger on, and the politician. As a result, our taxes go higher and higher and our spending and savings power goes lower and lower. The tragedy is that half of the money we give to the government to run things for us is wasted. So your responsibility is to locate those political hopefuls that will be efficient in running your government, watch how they perform and vote them out if they prove to be ineffective. Our federal government has become a safe haven for these hangers on who are able to stay in office even though they have done a terrible job of managing your money and your country. The result has been that the government has been poorly run, the expenditures are out of control, our reputation in the world community is abhorrent, and our elected officials simply blame the other guy or the other party.

If these parasites worked for a commercial, non-government entity they wouldn't last three months. Instead, some end up being reelected for a lifetime. For example, Senators currently, are paid $169,300.00 per year plus all the special privileges and perks they receive. When they retire they are paid the same salary for the rest of their lives. If a senator dies before his or her spouse the spouse continues to earn the same amount for the rest of his or her life. Meanwhile, if you live that long you will receive a meager pittance from the Social Security program-a pittance that you receive after paying into the program your entire working life. In contrast, a senator may be elected for only a short time but still receives his or her retirement. It is important to note here that your senators and congressmen do not participate in the Social Security program. This is not a worthy arrangement for people of their high elevation. An example of this is Senator Byrd, who can expect to draw over $7,000,000.00 in his retirement package. Senators and Representatives pay nothing ($0) into their retirement packages. Your elected officials still get their retirement packages even if they are convicted of crimes.

You can expect from Social Security somewhere around $12,000.00 per year on the average after you and your employer pay into it for your entire working life. This is another reason you should vote. This is also the reason you should write to your elected officials and tell them your desires on fiscal and other issues.

Members of the House of Representatives are paid $150,000.00 per year and the Speaker of the House is paid $192,000.00. They also receive funds to cover the costs of staff, postage, operation expenses and rental of offices in their home states.

You may wonder why this book has focused so much on taxes and fiscal matters.

By considering the following Budget of the U.S. Government for 2008 you will more fully understand why your vote is so important when it comes to our governments spending. The following is a list of most of the items from the 2008 budget. A complete copy is available to you for $39.00 from the Superintendent of Documents, PO Box 371954, Pittsburgh, PA 15260.

All amounts are in **BILLIONS** of dollars.

Dept of Agriculture $89,030,000,000.00
Dept of Commerce $3,812,000,000.00
Dept of Defense $538,283,000,000.00
Dept of Education......................$87,886,000,000.00
Dept of Energy.............................$3,620,000,000.00
Dept of Health $700,980,000,000.00
Dept of Homeland Sec.................$43,212,000,000.00
Dept of Housing..........................$92,131,000,000.00
Dept of Interior $10,792,000,000.00
Dept of Justice $24,121,000,000.00
Dept of Labor.............................$52,304,000,000.00
Dept of State..............................$35,360,000,000.00
Dept of Transportation...............$67,032,000,000.00
Dept of Treasury........................$61,259,000,000.00
Dept of Vet. Affairs.....................$83,290,000,000.00
Army Corps of Eng.......................$6,501,000,000.00
Environmental Protection $7,778,000,000.00
NASA..$17,251,000,000.00
Nat'l Science Foundation $6,026,000,000.00
Small Business Admin...............$21,900,000,000.00

GRAND TOTAL $2,902,000,000,000.00

That's trillions of dollars folks! These expenditures are almost 2% more than the government expects to receive in income.

Since 1945 the US government has donated more than $1,200,000,000,000.00 (that's trillions) in foreign aid to other countries.

According to the United Nations Organization, these countries are still no better off than they were in 1980. Is your money being wasted?

CHAPTER SIX
Why It's Important To Vote

"Ask not what your nation can do for you, ask what you can do for your nation."

John F. Kennedy

By now it is hoped you are forming a picture of why it is so important that you vote. Because so few vote, a small group of special interest folks may get the government they want and you have no voice in the decisions being made on your behalf. In politics, minority interests typically are very organized and become a powerful voice that gets heard, demands action and, often, can be contrary to the welfare of the majority.

Benjamin Franklin said it clearly; "In free governments the rulers are the servants and the people their superiors and sovereigns." The real power should then be in the hands of the people by electing representatives who will properly act on their behalf.

Another possible result is that unessential expenditures by the state or federal governments may well occur, resulting in excessive taxation, again, because you did not participate. Voting is important when we all get out and do it. It means little in terms of good government if we abandon our responsibility to vote.

As a new voter, it is important that you gather as much information as possible about the candidates. This can be done by going online to the appropriate web site or blog, going to community meetings, and reading the newspaper articles. Should the candidate be running for re-election, you can check his or her voting record, which is public information. You must be very careful when analyzing aired or written news articles on candidates as they are usually very biased by the station, newspaper, or candidate for office.

Candidates often speak at public forums, and this is an opportunity for you to ask questions of the candidate to learn better what his or her positions are on specific issues. You could ask questions about the candidate's position on abortion, war, global environments, education, trade, taxation, local government issues, immigration, or any subject of interest to you.

You are also encouraged to write to the political candidates or those in office on questions concerning our government and issues of special concern to you. They welcome your inquiries and you may well receive a response. The writer has written presidents, congressmen, senators and others in the government and has always received a response. It has not always been the reply he was looking for, but, a reply nonetheless. The following is a copy of a letter to Ronald Reagan and his response while he was Governor of California.

Anthony N. English
1712 Grenadier Dr.
San Pedro, California

May 18, 1967

Governor Ronald Reagan

Sacramento, California

Dear Governor Reagan:

I had the occasion to watch you on the television program: "Town Meeting of the World" this week, and I wish to complement you on the manner in which you represented our country.

There is little doubt in my mind that your attitude and leadership abilities dictate that you should seek the office of the President of the United States.

The future freedom of our country as well as the future freedom of the world is dependant upon leadership such as yours, to step forth and take the responsibility. You can count on my vote.

Very truly yours,

A..N. English

Anthony N. English

RONALD REAGAN
GOVERNOR

State of California

GOVERNOR'S OFFICE
SACRAMENTO 95814

June 14, 1967

Mr. Anthony N. English
1712 Grenadier Drive
San Pedro, California

Dear Mr. English:

I am indeed gratified that you would write me regarding
"Town Meeting of the World".

Thank you for your support and your concern about the
image of our country. It is inspiring to know that most
Americans maintain their traditional faith and pride
in our country.

Sincerely,

RONALD REAGAN
Governor

What are some of the worst things you can do as a voter? First, many people will just take a list from a newspaper and mark their ballots accordingly. This is folly, as the newspaper you take may be extremely liberal or left wing or ultra conservative and may be supporting candidates contrary to your own beliefs. Newspapers do not know better than you who should hold office. They are usually pushing a favored candidate to support their own interests.

Another big mistake voters make is in voting the way their boss or parents do. Times change and a country needs change as well so it is important that you have a mind of your own when casting your very important vote.

The other problem the voters have is all the advertisements and brochures that are received during election times. Most of these are a result of huge contributions by special interests groups or individuals and don't necessarily honestly represent the politician's course of action if elected. Read these with a jaundiced eye and dig deeper for the facts. You will find that many of these printed missiles are out and out lies to make you think if a certain bill or program fails it will be costly to you, the taxpayer. Usually the opposite is true. Many propositions presented to the voter are opposite to what they appear. A yes vote can be against an issue and a no vote can be for it. Analyze the presentations carefully.

You must consider, then, that when wealthy contributors, whether businesses or private persons, donate, huge sums of money to a politician, they are going to expect a return from their investment. The return comes to them in the form of your tax dollars, which are then distributed to the supporter in the form of lucrative contracts or cushy federal or state jobs.

A good example of this is when you hear a politician propose increasing taxes on corporations. This is a true con job against the taxpayer, as corporations do not pay taxes. When you increase the tax on a corporation the company then increases the price of the products it sells to you, so you end up paying the increased tax. Often, the result of increasing a corporation's tax is a reduction in sales of its products and, subsequently, a loss of jobs.

Sometimes there are special interest groups that are pushing a cause that will benefit only them. This is another reason why your vote is so important and why you should research the issue.

Your research is especially important because you will receive advertising mailers from the candidates. The candidate will send a brochure extolling his or her many virtues, experience and abilities. The opposition will send you a brochure showing that he or she is negligent, a crook, failed to show for political meetings, voting sessions and has been involved in shady schemes.

Only a thorough investigation on your part will help you decide who may be the right candidate.

CHAPTER SEVEN
Why Should You Vote

"Every government interference in the economy consists of giving an unearned benefit, extorted by force, to some at the expense of others."

Ayn Rand

Every national election results in the spending of hundreds of millions of dollars in order for a candidate to get elected. In the last three months, as preparation for the 2008 presidential election, several candidates have raised over $25,000,000.00. And this is just for openers. A political party will spend as much as $500 million to get its candidate elected.

The problem with this is that there are many special interest donors who are going to expect something in return for the money they have donated. For donations to be fair, there would have to be a law that only individual voters could donate to a candidate. This way, candidates would be beholden to the voter and not to special interest groups, unions, large corporations, or individual, wealthy donors. Large sums of money are not given to politicians because the donor thinks this person is the best candidate for the job. Organizations give large sums of money so they will get the voting support they want from the Congress or Senate when their special interest comes up.

What are special interests? A good example is farm subsidies. This was a program originally established to aid the small family farm following the depression era and the Oklahoma drought period. However, it has turned into a multi- billion-dollar annual gift to some of the largest farming corporations in America. As ridiculous as it may seem, very wealthy entertainers, newscasters, and other non-farming but wealthy people who have purchased large rural areas are receiving these same subsidies even though no real or productive farming is done on their "farms."

David Rockefeller, of the very wealthy Rockefeller family, received, in 2001 more than $134,000.00 not to farm his land. Scottie Pippen, star of the Portland Trailblazers basketball team received $26,000.00 not to farm his land. Even Bob Dole, retired US Senator and a very wealthy individual, received $6019.00. Ted Turner, the 25th richest man in America, received $12,925.00 for his farming interests.

This boondoggle will tax every working American about $4000.00 over the next ten years to provide subsidies to millionaires and profitable corporate farms.

There is no longer any reason for farm subsidies, but every year your elected politicians vote to award these gifts to these "farmers" in return for enough money to aid their own election process. Then the farmers return huge portions of money to those politicians they think will keep this program going.

This year congress proposed farm subsidies of $286,000,000,000.00. That's 286 BILLION dollars of your tax money.

Another example of special interest is companies that contract to the US government. Recently, in San Diego, California, a defense contractor was convicted of bribing former Representative, Randy "Duke" Cunningham (R) in exchange for $90 million dollars of Pentagon contracts. The congressman pled guilty to accepting $2.4 million in bribes. This is an all too common situation. It would seem to follow that if we vote with more knowledge of the candidates we could elect a more efficient government.

As these political parties spend hundreds of millions of dollars on the effort to get their candidates elected, one of their primary arguments is that they are doing all this for the underprivileged, the poor, and the disenfranchised. This is a consistent political theme in every presidential election in this century. You are to believe the candidate, if elected, is going to eliminate hunger, homelessness and despair. The only thing that happens when they do get elected is that trillions of dollars are spent by the bureaucrats and nothing changes except that many who would work for their survival learn to stay at home and live on the government dole. Some people are helped, but not nearly as many as the funds spent would indicate.

The political candidates go on to imply that only their party is interested in helping the underprivileged and the poor. This, of course, is also a falsehood. It has been shown that a great number of people from many walks of life or any party are very interested in helping those in need.

Natural calamities such as Katrina and other world wide natural tragedies have demonstrated the generosity of so many people throughout the universe. Facts have actually proven that the Conservative and Republicans are far more generous with their donations and giving than are their Liberal brethren.

This is why you must vote

Only you can help create an efficient and well organized government. Only you can stop the insidious waste of your hard earned-money. Only you can help create the government Americans deserve.

However, if you vote the same way so many have done in the past nothing will change. You will simply be electing ineffective, self serving "good old boys" (and girls) into the generous public trough, supported by your tax dollars.

President Harry Truman had a unique attitude regarding politicians and their interests in personal financial returns. When he retired from office in

1952, his income was, for the most part, a U.S. Army pension of $13,507.00 per year. Congress had observed that he was purchasing his own stamps, and licking them with his own tongue, so he was granted an allowance and, later, a pension of $25,000.00 per year.

He was offered corporate positions at quite large salaries but declined saying *"you don't want me. You want the office of the president, and that doesn't belong to me. It belongs to the American people and it's not for sale."*

About May 6, 1971 Congress was planning to award him the Medal of Freedom on his 87th birthday, he would not accept it, saying, "I don't consider that I have done anything which should be the reason for any award, Congressional or otherwise."

President Truman once said "My choice early in life was either to be a piano player in a house of ill repute or a politician. And to tell the truth, there is hardly any difference. I, for one, believe the piano player job to be much more honorable than current politicians."

Today our former presidents and other politicians use their past office credentials to make millions of dollars giving speeches, sitting on corporate boards and attaching their names to various programs, many times at the expense of the American voter.

CHAPTER EIGHT
The Electoral College

"You can fool all of the people some of the time, and some of the people all of the time, but you can't fool all of the people all of the time."

Abraham Lincoln

What is the Electoral College?

The final formality of selecting the president and vice-president was established by our early framers as covered by the articles of the US Constitution as outlined below. When you vote for a president, you are really voting to instruct the electors from your state to cast their votes for the same candidate.

An Elector cannot be a senator, a representative, or a person holding an office of trust or profit for the United States.

The electors are selected by the parties and are generally nominated by their state party committee. These electors are generally required to vote as the popular vote indicates so your vote is still significant. However, since the start of our formal government there has been only six times that a delegate did not vote as the popular vote dictated. There are as many electoral voters as there are senators and representatives from each state. These numbers are based on the population levels or by vote of the party's central Committees of the states as determined by the most recent census. Currently, there 538 Electoral College voters, and the majority needed to elect is 270.

Where did the term "Electoral College" originate?

Our founders copied the idea from the Holy Roman Empire system of the era 962-1806. They used a system of princes from various German States authorized to vote for the election of the German King. The term "college" comes from the Latin "collegium" referring to a body of people acting as a unit.

Electoral College Votes by State

State	Electors	Percentage of Electors	Population	Percentage of Population
Alabama	9	1.67%	4,461,130	1.58%
Alaska	3	0.56%	628,933	0.22%
Arizona	10	1.86%	5,140,683	1.82%
Arkansas	6	1.12%	2,679,733	0.95%
California	55	10.22%	33,930,798	12.03%
Colorado	9	1.67%	4,311,882	1.53%
Connecticut	7	1.30%	3,409,535	1.21%
Delaware	3	0.56%	785,068	0.28%
District of Columbia	3	0.56%	574,096	0.20%
Florida	27	5.02%	16,028,890	5.68%
Georgia	15	2.79%	8,206,975	2.91%
Hawaii	4	0.74%	1,216,642	0.43%
Idaho	4	0.74%	1,297,274	0.46%
Illinois	21	3.90%	12,439,042	4.41%
Indiana	11	2.04%	6,090,782	2.16%
Iowa	7	1.30%	2,931,923	1.04%
Kansas	6	1.12%	2,693,824	0.96%
Kentucky	8	1.49%	4,049,431	1.44%
Louisiana	9	1.67%	4,480,271	1.59%
Maine	4	0.74%	1,277,731	0.45%
Maryland	10	1.86%	5,307,886	1.88%
Massachusetts	12	2.23%	6,355,568	2.25%
Michigan	17	3.16%	9,955,829	3.53%

Minnesota	10	1.86%	4,925,670	1.75%
Mississippi	6	1.12%	2,852,927	1.01%
Missouri	11	2.04%	5,606,260	1.99%
Montana	3	0.56%	905,316	0.32%
Nebraska	5	0.93%	1,715,369	0.61%
Nevada	5	0.93%	2,002,032	0.71%
New Hampshire	4	0.74%	1,238,415	0.44%
New Jersey	15	2.79%	8,424,354	2.99%
New Mexico	5	0.93%	1,823,821	0.65%
New York	31	5.76%	19,004,973	6.74%
North Carolina	15	2.79%	8,067,673	2.86%
North Dakota	3	0.56%	643,756	0.23%
Ohio	20	3.72%	11,374,540	4.03%
Oklahoma	7	1.30%	3,458,819	1.23%
Oregon	7	1.30%	3,428,543	1.22%
Pennsylvania	21	3.90%	12,300,670	4.36%
Rhode Island	4	0.74%	1,049,662	0.37%
South Carolina	8	1.49%	4,025,061	1.43%
South Dakota	3	0.56%	756,874	0.27%
Tennessee	11	2.04%	5,700,037	2.02%
Texas	34	6.32%	20,903,994	7.41%
Utah	5	0.93%	2,236,714	0.79%
Vermont	3	0.56%	609,890	0.22%
Virginia	13	2.42%	7,100,702	2.52%
Washington	11	2.04%	5,908,684	2.10%
West Virginia	5	0.93%	1,813,077	0.64%
Wisconsin	10	1.86%	5,371,210	1.90%
Wyoming	3	0.56%	495,304	0.18%
Totals	**538**	**100.00%**		**100.00**

CHAPTER NINE
Important Issues to Consider

"Government is not your Daddy"

Marilyn English

Who is more responsible for the money that the government spends? Is it the president or the Congress?

While the president as the head of the government will be responsible for whatever happens under his watch, it is the Congress who is actually spending the money. This means that to really effect change it is more important to have a Congress of men and women that will be looking out for your interests than it is a president. They really control the purse strings and are the ones responsible for the excessive spending that continues to go on. They regularly add pork barrel, or so called "line item" expenditures to necessary programs so that their contributing donors can get some juicy federal contracts. Therefore, if you really want to improve things you need to vote out those pork barrel congressmen who are causing the problem and vote in new, responsible, honest, and trustworthy men and women.

Another consideration is taxes. Right now the tax structure is such that the more income you earn the higher your tax rate. The only problem with this is that at the same time congress is setting tax rates, especially on the rich, they have set a huge number of tax write offs, resulting in many rich earners paying a very low amount and in some case nothing at all while the middle class picks up the bulk of the tax load.

There have been proposed several new ideas for a tax structure that would be more fair to all Americans. One is to have a flat tax for all earners. Possibly very low earners, $30,000 per year or less could be exempt from income taxes. Everyone else would pay a flat rate on any income over $30,000.00 per year. No one would get a write off. If, for example, the tax rate was set at 15%, someone who earns $1,000,000.00 would pay $150,000.00 and someone who earns $100,000.00 would pay $15,000.00. The government would collect more income than it does now, and the returns you file would be very simple.

Another national tax idea that has been proposed to replace the income tax is a National sales tax. This is a tax that would be placed on purchases made by consumers and users. For example, if one purchases a television set, a lamp or a set of dishes a tax would be added that goes to the federal government. People who purchase things would pay the tax. People who buy lots of things would pay more tax. At least on the surface, this system seems to have some merit.

In both cases this would also mean that the IRS could be reduced to one tenth of the size it is now, saving our government hundreds of millions of dollars. The general consensus is that the existing IRS system is very cumbersome, very expensive and, very unfair.

The only real opponents to a simplified tax system are your elected officials who want more of your money, the IRS, and the accountants who prepare the income tax returns at great expense to the taxpayer. Even Albert Einstein, one of the world's greatest minds observed *"The hardest thing in the world to understand is the income tax."*

Your vote could change this system!

The other item of great importance is subsidies. Tremendous sums of money are sent to foreign countries. Little of it actually gets down to the people in need. Instead, it is retained by the dictators, despots, and government officials who end up using the funds for their own benefits.

In addition to your money being wasted and given without fiscal regard to foreign entities these same elected politicians with stupid disregard for your hard earned dollars waste money at the domestic level like drunken lottery winners.

Our government erroneously paid out more than $19 billion to the Medicare program in 2004 due to fraud and waste.

Millions have been lost because the government issued personal credit cards to employees to facilitate purchases of needed supplies. The only problem is they discovered millions of dollars have been charged for tickets to sporting events, tickets to plays, purchases of lingerie and other personal items.

The "Creative Wellness" program was set up at a cost of over $1,000,000.00 to teach public tenants how to burn incense. You are paying for all of this in your taxes.

These are only a drop in the bucket to all the ridiculous line item expenditures your congress spends money on. Check it out on- line and you will be astounded by the facts. This is why you must vote intelligently if you want a better government.

Many politicians running for office today harp on our need to change, but what really needs to be changed are the members of the House of Representatives and the Senate who are, unquestionably, the guilty parties responsible for our fiscal mess.

On May 19, 2008 it was announced that our federal deficit was $61,700,000,000,000. That, once again, is trillions of dollars. What this means to you is that you have a deficit of $531,472 per household here in America. Included in these numbers are civil servant retirement packages of $106,000,000,000.00. That's billions. So what this means is that for all the people who are working for our "government" you are paying for their retirement package after paying their income for their entire career. That is the equivalent of a mortgage on a house you may be buying or expect to buy. But is nothing more than funds you, as a family, will have to pay sooner or later to get your government out of dept. The rich won't pay this, the politicians won't pay this. Pay attention-you and your family will pay this because we have elected so many ineffective politicians to our congress and our senate. This is an indisputable fact. The solution is very simple. Clean out the house and the senate and elect credible, professional and moral people to our government.

There is always too much credit or blame placed on the president for the various conditions that occur from a national standpoint. Presidents can't make as much happen as you may wish to think. Certainly they can lead and they can suggest and they can encourage. Presidents can cajole the senate and the house into looking into proposed activities and expenditures but presidents can't make it happen. Congress and the senate are the movers and shakers of what laws are passed and what monies are spent. If a president could change things there would never be a recession. He or she would simply stop it if they could. He or she can't. If a president could institute national health care he or she would just do it. They can't.

As the major elections develop and we are bombasted with the rhetoric of the candidates you can expect to receive so many promotional and advertising blurbs on the merits of the various candidates as well as all their failings as far as their opposition is concerned. Most of these mailings are indecipherable and erroneous and you need to read each and every one with a special caution because there is a very great likelihood that they are totally false.

You are now challenged to vote with "passion, purpose and power." Exercise your voter's rights and make America an even better place for you, your children and your grandchildren.

CHAPTER TEN
The US Constitution

"No man's life, liberty or property are safe while the Congress is in session."

Mark Twain

The following is the Constitution of the United States of America and the Preamble to the constitution. There is very little argument that it is probably the most well written, most perceptive and most meaningful outline of a government to represent the freedoms and rights of human beings than anything that has ever been published in the entire history of mankind.

It is hoped that you will read this and it is believed that ,once read, your concept of what life , liberty, citizenship and the pursuit of happiness really means will become a foundation for your life and the lives of your families.

- U.S. Constitution
  Article II
  Section 1
  Amendment XII
  Amendment XX
- U.S. Code, Title 3, section 15
- Precedents of the House of Representatives
- Overview of the Electoral College System

U.S. Constitution
Article II
Section 1

Section 1. The executive power shall be vested in a President of the United States of America. He shall hold his office during the term of four years, and, together with the Vice President, chosen for the same term, be elected, as follows: Each state shall appoint, in such manner as the Legislature thereof may direct, a number of electors, equal to the whole number of Senators and Representatives to which the State may be entitled in the Congress: but no Senator or Representative, or person holding an office of trust or profit under the United States, shall be appointed an elector. The electors shall meet in their respective states, and vote by ballot for two persons, of whom one at least shall not be an inhabitant of the same state with themselves. And they shall make a list of all the persons voted for, and of the number of votes for each; which list they shall sign and certify, and transmit sealed to the seat of the government of the United States, directed to the President of the Senate. The President of the Senate shall, in the presence of the Senate and House of Representatives, open all the certificates, and the votes shall then be counted. The person having the greatest number of votes shall be the President, if such number be a majority of the whole number of electors appointed; and if there be more than one who have such majority, and have an equal number of votes, then the House of Representatives shall immediately choose by ballot one of them for President; and if no person have a majority, then

49

from the five highest on the list the said House shall in like manner choose the President. But in choosing the President, the votes shall be taken by States, the representation from each state having one vote; A quorum for this purpose shall consist of a member or members from two thirds of the states, and a majority of all the states shall be necessary to a choice. In every case, after the choice of the President, the person having the greatest number of votes of the electors shall be the Vice President. But if there should remain two or more who have equal votes, the Senate shall choose from them by ballot the Vice President. The Congress may determine the time of choosing the electors, and the day on which they shall give their votes; which day shall be the same throughout the United States. No person except a natural born citizen, or a citizen of the United States, at the time of the adoption of this Constitution, shall be eligible to the office of President; neither shall any person be eligible to that office who shall not have attained to the age of thirty five years, and been fourteen Years a resident within the United States. In case of the removal of the President from office, or of his death, resignation, or inability to discharge the powers and duties of the said office, the same shall devolve on the Vice President, and the Congress may by law provide for the case of removal, death, resignation or inability, both of the President and Vice President, declaring what officer shall then act as President, and such officer shall act accordingly, until the disability be removed, or a President shall be elected. The President shall, at stated times, receive for his services, a compensation, which shall neither be increased nor diminished during the period for which he shall have been elected, and he shall not receive within that period any other emolument from the United States, or any of them. Before he enter on the execution of his office, he shall take the following oath or affirmation:--"I do solemnly swear (or affirm) that I will faithfully execute the office of President of the United States, and will to the best of my ability, preserve, protect and defend the Constitution of the United States."

Amendment XII

The electors shall meet in their respective states and vote by ballot for President and Vice-President, one of whom, at least, shall not be an inhabitant of the same state with themselves; they shall name in their ballots the person voted for as President, and in distinct ballots the person voted for as Vice-President, and they shall make distinct lists of all persons voted for as President, and of all persons voted for as Vice-President, and of the number of votes for each, which lists they shall sign and certify, and transmit sealed to the seat of the government of the United States, directed to the President of the Senate;--The President of the Senate shall, in the presence of the Senate and House of Representatives, open all the certificates and the votes shall then be counted;--the person having the greatest number of votes for President, shall be the President, if such number be a majority of the whole number of electors appointed; and if no person have such majority, then from the persons having the highest numbers not exceeding three on the list of those voted for as President, the House of Representatives shall choose immediately, by ballot, the President. But in choosing the President, the votes shall be taken by states, the representation from each state having one vote; a quorum for this purpose shall consist of a member or members from two-thirds of the states and a majority of all the states shall be necessary to a choice. And if the House of Representatives shall not choose a President whenever the right of choice shall devolve upon them, before the fourth day of March next following, then the Vice-President shall act as President, as in the case of the death or other constitutional disability of the President. The person having the greatest number of votes as Vice-President, shall be the Vice-President, if such number be a majority of the whole number of electors appointed, and if no person have a majority, then from the two highest numbers on the list, the Senate shall choose the Vice-President; a quorum for the purpose shall consist of two-thirds of the whole number of Senators, and a majority of the whole number shall be necessary to a choice. But no person constitutionally ineligible to the office of President shall be eligible to that of Vice-President of the United States.

Amendment XX

Section 1. The terms of the President and Vice President shall end at noon on the 20th day of January, and the terms of Senators and Representatives at noon on the 3d day of January, of the years in which such terms would have ended if this article had not been ratified; and the terms of their successors shall then begin. Section 2. The Congress shall assemble at least once in every year, and such meeting shall begin at noon on the 3d day of January, unless they shall by law appoint a different day. Section 3. If, at the time fixed for the beginning of the term of the President, the President elect shall have died, the Vice President elect shall become President. If a President shall not have been chosen before the time fixed for the beginning of his term, or if the President elect shall have failed to qualify, then the Vice President elect shall act as President until a President shall have qualified; and the Congress may by law provide for the case wherein neither a President elect nor a Vice President elect shall have qualified, declaring who shall then act as President, or the manner in which one who is to act shall be selected, and such person shall act accordingly until a President or Vice President shall have qualified. Section 4. The Congress may by law provide for the case of the death of any of the persons from whom the House of Representatives may choose a President whenever the right of choice shall have devolved upon them, and for the case of the death of any of the persons from whom the Senate may choose a Vice President whenever the right of choice shall have devolved upon them. Section 5. Sections 1 and 2 shall take effect on the 15th day of October following the ratification of this article. Section 6. This article shall be inoperative unless it shall have been ratified as an amendment to the Constitution by the legislatures of three-fourths of the several states within seven years from the date of its submission.

U.S. Code
Title 3, section 15
Counting Electoral Votes in Congress

Congress shall be in session on the sixth day of January succeeding every meeting of the electors. The Senate and House of Representatives shall meet in the Hall of the House of Representatives at the hour of 1 o'clock in the afternoon on that day, and the President of the Senate shall be their presiding officer. Two tellers shall be previously appointed on the part of the Senate and two on the part of the House of Representatives, to whom shall be handed, as they are opened by the President of the Senate, all the certificates and papers purporting to be certificates of the electoral votes, which certificates and papers shall be opened, presented, and acted upon in the alphabetical order of the States, beginning with the letter A; and said tellers, having then read the same in the presence and hearing of the two Houses, shall make a list of the votes as they shall appear from the said certificates; and the votes having been ascertained and counted according to the rules in this subchapter provided, the result of the same shall be delivered to the President of the Senate, who shall thereupon announce the state of the vote, which announcement shall be deemed a sufficient declaration of the persons, if any, elected President and Vice President of the United States, and, together with a list of votes, be entered on the Journals of the two Houses. Upon such reading of any such certificate or paper, the President of the Senate shall call for objections, if any. Every objection shall be made in writing, and shall state clearly and concisely, and without argument, the ground thereof, and shall be signed by at least one Senator and one Member of the House of Representatives before the same shall be received. When all objections so made to any vote or paper from a State shall have been received and read, the Senate shall thereupon withdraw, and such objections shall be submitted to the Senate for its decision; and the Speaker of the House of Representatives shall, in like manner, submit such objections to the House of Representatives for its decision; and no electoral vote or votes from any State which shall have been regularly given by electors whose appointment has been lawfully certified to according to section 6 of this title from which but one return has been received shall be rejected, but the two Houses concurrently may reject the vote or votes when they agree that such vote or votes have not been so regularly given by electors whose appointment has been so certified. If more than one return or paper purporting to be a return from a State shall have been received by the President of the Senate, those votes, and those only, shall be counted which shall have been regularly given by the electors who are shown by the determination mentioned in section 5 of this title to have been appointed, if the determination in said section provided for shall have been made, or by such successors or substitutes, in case of a vacancy in the board of electors so ascertained, as have been appointed to fill such vacancy in the mode provided by the laws of the State, but in case there shall arise the question which of two or more of such State authorities determining what electors have been appointed, as mentioned in section 5 of this title, is the lawful tribunal of such State, the votes regularly given of those electors, and those only, of such State shall be counted whose title as electors the two Houses, acting separately, shall concurrently decide is supported by the decision of such State so authorized by its law; and in such case of more than one return or paper purporting to be a return from a State, if there shall have been no such determination of the question in the State aforesaid, then those votes, and those only, shall be counted which the two Houses shall concurrently decide were cast by lawful electors appointed in accordance with the laws of the State, unless the two Houses, acting separately, shall concurrently decide such votes not to be the lawful votes of the legally appointed electors of such State. But if the two Houses shall disagree in respect of the counting of such votes, then, and in that case, the votes of the electors whose appointment shall have been certified by the executive of the State, under the seal thereof, shall be counted. When the two Houses have voted, they shall immediately again meet, and the presiding officer shall then announce the decision of the questions submitted. No votes or papers from any other State shall be acted upon until the objections previously made to the votes or papers from any State shall have been finally disposed of.

Presidential Election by the House

*Excerpted from Congressional Quarterly, Inc., **Presidential Elections Since 1789**, Fifth Edition p. 226. These rules were adopted by the House in 1825 to decide the presidential election of 1824. They con-*

tinue to provide the precedent for any presidential election thrown into the House; however, the House could change these rules at any time.

1. In the event of its appearing, on opening all the certificates, and counting the votes given by the electors of the several States for President, that no person has a majority of the votes of the whole number of electors appointed, the same shall be entered on the Journals of this House.

2. The roll of the House shall then be called by States; and, on its appearing that a Member or Members from two-thirds of the States are present, the House shall immediately proceed, by ballot, to choose a President from the persons having the highest numbers, not exceeding three, on the list of those voted for as President; and, in case neither of those persons shall receive the votes of a majority of all the states on the first ballot, the House shall continue to ballot for a President, without interruption by other business, until a President be chosen.

3. The doors of the Hall shall be closed during the balloting, except against the Members of the Senate, stenographers, and the officers of the House.

4. From the commencement of the balloting until an election is made no proposition to adjourn shall be received, unless on the motion

of one State, seconded by States. The same rule shall be observed in regard to any motion to change the usual hour for the meeting of the House.

5. In balloting the following mode shall be observed, to wit:

    i. The Representatives of each State shall be arranged and seated together, beginning with the seats at the right hand of the Speaker's chair, with the Members from the State of Maine; thence, proceeding with the Members from the States, in the order the States are usually named for receiving petitions around the Hall of the House, until all are seated.

    ii. A ballot box shall be provided for each State.

    iii. The Representatives of each State shall, in the first instance, ballot among themselves, in order to ascertain the vote of their State; and they may, if necessary, appoint tellers of their ballots.

    iv. After the vote of each State is ascertained, duplicates thereof shall be made out; and in case any one of the persons from whom the choice is to be made shall receive a majority of the votes given, on any one balloting by the Representatives of a State, the name of that person shall be written on each of the duplicates; and in case the votes so given shall be divided so that neither of said persons shall have a majority of the whole number of votes given by such State, on any one balloting, then the word "divided" shall be written on each duplicate.

v. After the delegation from each State shall have ascertained the vote of their State, the Clerk shall name the States in the order they are usually named for receiving petitions; and as the name of each is called the Sergeant-at Arms shall present to the delegation of each two ballot boxes, in each of which shall be deposited, by some Representative of the State, one of the duplicates made as aforesaid of the vote of said State, in the presence and subject to the examination of all the Members from said State then present; and where there is more than one Representative from a State, the duplicates shall not both be deposited by the same person.

vi. When the votes of the States are thus all taken in, the Sergeant-at-Arms shall carry one of said ballot boxes to one table and the other to a separate and distinct table.

vii. One person from each State represented in the balloting shall be appointed by the Representatives to tell off said ballots; but, in case the Representatives fail to appoint a teller, the Speaker shall appoint.

viii.   The said tellers shall divide themselves into two sets, as nearly equal in number as can be, and one of the said sets of tellers shall proceed to count the votes in one of said boxes, and the other set the votes in the other box.

ix. When the votes are counted by the different sets of tellers, the result shall be reported to the House; and if the reports agree, the same shall be accepted as the true votes of the States; but if the reports disagree, the States shall proceed, in the same manner as before, to a new ballot.

6.   All questions arising after the balloting commences, requiring the decision of the House, which shall be decided by the House, voting per capita, to be incidental to the power of choosing a President, shall be decided by States without debate; and in case of an equal division of the votes of States, the question shall be lost.

7.   When either of the persons from whom the choice is to be made shall have received a majority of all the States, the Speaker shall declare the same, and that that person is elected President of the United States.

8. The result shall be immediately communicated to the Senate by message, and a committee of three persons shall be appointed to inform the President of the United States and the President-elect of said election.

The election of John Quincy Adams was decided in accordance with these regulations on Feb 9, 1825.

Article. I. - The Legislative Branch

Section 1 - The Legislature

All legislative Powers herein granted shall be vested in a Congress of the United States, which shall consist of a Senate and House of Representatives.

Section 2 - The House

The House of Representatives shall be composed of Members chosen every second Year by the People of the several States, and the Electors in each State shall have the Qualifications requisite for Electors of the most numerous Branch of the State Legislature.

No Person shall be a Representative who shall not have attained to the Age of twenty five Years, and been seven Years a Citizen of the United States, and who shall not, when elected, be an Inhabitant of that State in which he shall be chosen.

(Representatives and direct Taxes shall be apportioned among the several States which may be included within this Union, according to their respective Numbers, which shall be determined by adding to the whole Number of free Persons, including those bound to Service for a Term of Years, and excluding Indians not taxed, three fifths of all other Persons.) **(The previous sentence in parentheses was modified by the 14th Amendment, section 2.)** The actual Enumeration shall be made within three Years after the first Meeting of the Congress of the United States, and within every subsequent Term of ten Years, in such Manner as they shall by Law direct. The Number of Representatives shall not exceed one for every thirty Thousand, but each State shall have at Least one Representative; and until such enumeration shall be made, the State of New Hampshire shall be entitled to choose three, Massachusetts eight, Rhode Island and Providence Plantations one, Connecticut five, New York six, New Jersey four, Pennsylvania eight, Delaware one, Maryland six, Virginia ten, North Carolina five, South Carolina five and Georgia three.

When vacancies happen in the Representation from any State, the Executive Authority thereof shall issue Writs of Election to fill such Vacancies.

The House of Representatives shall choose their Speaker and other Officers; and shall have the sole Power of Impeachment.

Section 3 - The Senate

The Senate of the United States shall be composed of two Senators from each State, (chosen by the Legislature thereof,) **(The preceding words in pa-**

rentheses superseded by 17th Amendment, section 1.) for six Years; and each Senator shall have one Vote.

Immediately after they shall be assembled in Consequence of the first Election, they shall be divided as equally as may be into three Classes. The Seats of the Senators of the first Class shall be vacated at the Expiration of the second Year, of the second Class at the Expiration of the fourth Year, and of the third Class at the Expiration of the sixth Year, so that one third may be chosen every second Year; *(and if Vacancies happen by Resignation, or otherwise, during the Recess of the Legislature of any State, the Executive thereof may make temporary Appointments until the next Meeting of the Legislature, which shall then fill such Vacancies.)* **(The preceding words in parentheses were superseded by the 17th Amendment, section 2.)**

No person shall be a Senator who shall not have attained to the Age of thirty Years, and been nine Years a Citizen of the United States, and who shall not, when elected, be an Inhabitant of that State for which he shall be chosen.

The Vice President of the United States shall be President of the Senate, but shall have no Vote, unless they be equally divided.

The Senate shall choose their other Officers, and also a President pro tempore, in the absence of the Vice President, or when he shall exercise the Office of President of the United States.

The Senate shall have the sole Power to try all Impeachments. When sitting for that Purpose, they shall be on Oath or Affirmation. When the President of the United States is tried, the Chief Justice shall preside: And no Person shall be convicted without the Concurrence of two thirds of the Members present.

Judgment in Cases of Impeachment shall not extend further than to removal from Office, and disqualification to hold and enjoy any Office of honor, Trust or Profit under the United States: but the Party convicted shall nevertheless be liable and subject to Indictment, Trial, Judgment and Punishment, according to Law.

Section 4 - Elections, Meetings

The Times, Places and Manner of holding Elections for Senators and Representatives, shall be prescribed in each State by the Legislature thereof; but the Congress may at any time by Law make or alter such Regulations, except as to the Place of Choosing Senators.

The Congress shall assemble at least once in every Year, and such Meeting shall *(be on the first Monday in December,)* **(The preceding words in parentheses were superseded by the 20th Amendment, section 2.)** unless they shall by Law appoint a different Day.

Section 5 - Membership, Rules, Journals, Adjournment

Each House shall be the Judge of the Elections, Returns and Qualifications of its own Members, and a Majority of each shall constitute a Quorum to do Business; but a smaller number may adjourn from day to day, and may be authorized to compel the Attendance of absent Members, in such Manner, and under such Penalties as each House may provide.

Each House may determine the Rules of its Proceedings, punish its Members for disorderly Behavior, and, with the Concurrence of two-thirds, expel a Member.

Each House shall keep a Journal of its Proceedings, and from time to time publish the same, excepting such Parts as May in their Judgment require Secrecy; and the Yeas and Nays of the Members of either House on any question shall, at the Desire of one fifth of those Present, be entered on the Journal.

Neither House, during the Session of Congress, shall, without the Consent of the other, adjourn for more than three days, nor to any other Place than that in which the two Houses shall be sitting.

Section 6 - Compensation

(The Senators and Representatives shall receive a Compensation for their Services, to be ascertained by Law, and paid out of the Treasury of the United

States.) **(The preceding words in parentheses were modified by the 27th Amendment.)** They shall in all Cases, except Treason, Felony and Breach of the Peace, be privileged from Arrest during their Attendance at the Session of their respective Houses, and in going to and returning from the same; and for any Speech or Debate in either House, they shall not be questioned in any other Place.

No Senator or Representative shall, during the Time for which he was elected, be appointed to any civil Office under the Authority of the United States which shall have been created, or the Emoluments whereof shall have been increased during such time; and no Person holding any Office under the United States, shall be a Member of either House during his Continuance in Office.

Section 7 - Revenue Bills, Legislative Process, Presidential Veto

All bills for raising Revenue shall originate in the House of Representatives; but the Senate may propose or concur with Amendments as on other Bills.

Every Bill which shall have passed the House of Representatives and the Senate, shall, before it become a Law, be presented to the President of the United States; If he approve he shall sign it, but if not he shall return it, with his Objections to that House in which it shall have originated, who shall enter the Objections at large on their Journal, and proceed to reconsider it. If after such Reconsideration two thirds of that House shall agree to pass the Bill, it shall be sent, together with the Objections, to the other House, by which it shall likewise be reconsidered, and if approved by two thirds of that House, it shall become a Law. But in all such Cases the Votes of both Houses shall be determined by Yeas and Nays, and the Names of the Persons voting for and against the Bill shall be entered on the Journal of each House respectively. If any Bill shall not be returned by the President within ten Days (Sundays excepted) after it shall have been presented to him, the same shall be a Law, in like Manner as if he had signed it, unless the Congress by their Adjournment prevent its Return, in which Case it shall not be a Law.

Every Order, Resolution, or Vote to which the Concurrence of the Senate and House of Representatives may be necessary (except on a question of Adjournment) shall be presented to the President of the United States; and before the Same shall take Effect, shall be approved by him, or being disapproved by him, shall be repassed by two thirds of the Senate and House of Representatives, according to the Rules and Limitations prescribed in the Case of a Bill.

Section 8 - Powers of Congress

The Congress shall have Power To lay and collect Taxes, Duties, Imposts and Excises, to pay the Debts and provide for the common Defense and general Welfare of the United States; but all Duties,

Imposts and Excises shall be uniform throughout the United States;

To borrow money on the credit of the United States;

To regulate Commerce with foreign Nations, and among the several States, and with the Indian Tribes;

To establish an uniform Rule of Naturalization, and uniform Laws on the subject of Bankruptcies throughout the United States;

To coin Money, regulate the Value thereof, and of foreign Coin, and fix the Standard of Weights and Measures;

To provide for the Punishment of counterfeiting the Securities and current Coin of the United States;

To establish Post Offices and Post Roads;

To promote the Progress of Science and useful Arts, by securing for limited Times to Authors and Inventors the exclusive Right to their respective Writings and Discoveries;

To constitute Tribunals inferior to the Supreme Court;

To define and punish Piracies and Felonies committed on the high Seas, and Offenses against the Law of Nations;

To declare War, grant Letters of Marque and Reprisal, and make Rules concerning Captures on Land and Water;

To raise and support Armies, but no Appropriation of Money to that Use shall be for a longer Term than two Years;

To provide and maintain a Navy;

To make Rules for the Government and Regulation of the land and naval Forces;

To provide for calling forth the Militia to execute the Laws of the Union, suppress Insurrections and repel Invasions;

To provide for organizing, arming, and disciplining the Militia, and for governing such Part of them as may be employed in the Service of the United States, reserving to the States respectively, the Appointment of the Officers, and the Authority of training the Militia according to the discipline prescribed by Congress;

To exercise exclusive Legislation in all Cases whatsoever, over such District (not exceeding ten Miles square) as may, by Cession of particular States, and the acceptance of Congress, become the Seat of the Government of the United States, and to exercise like Authority over all Places purchased by the Consent of the Legislature of the State in which the Same shall be, for the Erection of Forts, Magazines,

Arsenals, dock-Yards, and other needful Buildings; And

To make all Laws which shall be necessary and proper for carrying into Execution the foregoing Powers, and all other Powers vested by this Constitution in the Government of the United States, or in any Department or Officer thereof.

Section 9 - Limits on Congress

The Migration or Importation of such Persons as any of the States now existing shall think proper to admit, shall not be prohibited by the Congress prior to the Year one thousand eight hundred and eight, but a tax or duty may be imposed on such Importation, not exceeding ten dollars for each Person.

The privilege of the Writ of Habeas Corpus shall not be suspended, unless when in Cases of Rebellion or Invasion the public Safety may require it.

No Bill of Attainder or ex post facto Law shall be passed.

(No capitation, or other direct, Tax shall be laid, unless in Proportion to the Census or Enumeration *herein before directed to be taken.)*

(Section in parentheses clarified by the 16th Amendment.)

No Tax or Duty shall be laid on Articles exported from any State.

No Preference shall be given by any Regulation of Commerce or Revenue to the Ports of one State over those of another: nor shall Vessels bound to, or from, one State, be obliged to enter, clear, or pay Duties in another.

No Money shall be drawn from the Treasury, but in Consequence of Appropriations made by Law; and a regular Statement and Account of the Receipts and Expenditures of all public Money shall be published from time to time.

No Title of Nobility shall be granted by the United States: And no Person holding any Office of Profit or Trust under them, shall, without the Consent of the Congress, accept of any present, Emolument, Office, or Title, of any kind whatever, from any King, Prince or foreign State.

Section 10 - Powers prohibited of States

No State shall enter into any Treaty, Alliance, or Confederation; grant Letters of Marque and Reprisal; coin Money; emit Bills of Credit; make any Thing but gold and silver Coin a Tender in Payment of Debts; pass any Bill of Attainder, ex post facto Law, or Law impairing the Obligation of Contracts, or grant any Title of Nobility.

No State shall, without the Consent of the Congress, lay any Imposts or Duties on Imports or Exports, except what may be absolutely necessary for executing it's inspection Laws: and the net Produce of all Duties and Imposts, laid by any State on Imports or

Exports, shall be for the Use of the Treasury of the United States; and all such Laws shall be subject to the Revision and Control of the Congress.

No State shall, without the Consent of Congress, lay any duty of Tonnage, keep Troops, or Ships of War in time of Peace, enter into any Agreement or Compact with another State, or with a foreign Power, or engage in War, unless actually invaded, or in such imminent Danger as will not admit of delay.

Article. II. - The Executive Branch

Section 1 - The President

The executive Power shall be vested in a President of the United States of America. He shall hold his Office during the Term of four Years, and, together with the Vice-President chosen for the same Term, be elected, as follows:

Each State shall appoint, in such Manner as the Legislature thereof may direct, a Number of Electors, equal to the whole Number of Senators and Representatives to which the State may be entitled in the Congress: but no Senator or Representative, or Person holding an Office of Trust or Profit under the United States, shall be appointed an Elector.

(The Electors shall meet in their respective States, and vote by Ballot for two persons, of whom one at least shall not lay an Inhabitant of the same State with themselves. And they shall make a List of all the Persons voted for, and of the Number of Votes for each; which List they shall sign and certify, and transmit sealed to the Seat of the Government of the United States, directed to the President of the Senate. The President of the Senate shall, in the Presence of the Senate and House of Representatives, open all the Certificates, and the Votes shall then be counted. The Person having the greatest Number of Votes shall be the President, if such Number be a Majority of the whole Number of Electors appointed; and if there be more than one who have such Majority, and have an equal Number of Votes, then the House of Representatives shall immediately choose by Ballot one of them for President; and if no Person have a Majority, then from the five highest on the List the said House shall in like Manner choose *the President. But in* choosing *the President, the Votes shall be taken by States, the Representation from each State having one Vote; a* quorum for this Purpose shall consist of a Member or Members from two-thirds of the States, and a Majority of all the States shall be necessary to a Choice. In every Case, after the Choice of the President, the Person having the greatest Number of Votes of the Electors shall be the Vice President. But if there should remain two or more who have equal Votes, the Senate shall choose *from them by Ballot the Vice-President.)* **(This clause in parentheses was superseded by the 12th Amendment.)**

The Congress may determine the Time of choosing the Electors, and the Day on which they shall give their Votes; which Day shall be the same throughout the United States.

No person except a natural born Citizen, or a Citizen of the United States, at the time of the Adoption of this Constitution, shall be eligible to the Office of President; neither shall any Person be eligible to that Office who shall not have attained to the Age of thirty-five Years, and been fourteen Years a Resident within the United States.

(In Case of the Removal of the President from Office, or of his Death, Resignation, or Inability to discharge the Powers and Duties of the said Office, the same shall devolve on the Vice President, and the Congress may by Law provide for the Case of Removal, Death, Resignation or Inability, both of the President and Vice President, declaring what Officer shall then act as President, and such Officer shall act accordingly, until the Disability be removed, or a President shall be elected.) **(This clause in parentheses has been modified by the 20th and 25th Amendments.)**

The President shall, at stated Times, receive for his Services, a Compensation, which shall neither be increased nor diminished during the Period for which he shall have been elected, and he shall not receive within that Period any other Emolument from the United States, or any of them.

Before he entered on the Execution of his Office, he shall take the following Oath or Affirmation:

"I do solemnly swear (or affirm) that I will faithfully execute the Office of President of the United States, and will to the best of my Ability, preserve, protect and defend the Constitution of the United States."

Section 2 - Civilian Power over Military, Cabinet, Pardon Power, Appointments

The President shall be Commander in Chief of the Army and Navy of the United States, and of the Militia of the several States, when called into the actual Service of the United States; he may require the Opinion, in writing, of the principal Officer in each of the executive Departments, upon any subject relating to the Duties of their respective Offices, and he shall have Power to Grant Reprieves and Pardons for Offenses against the United States, except in Cases of Impeachment.

He shall have Power, by and with the Advice and Consent of the Senate, to make Treaties, provided two thirds of the Senators present concur; and he shall nominate, and by and with the Advice and Consent of the Senate, shall appoint Ambassadors, other public Ministers and Consuls, Judges of the supreme Court, and all other Officers of the United States, whose Appointments are not herein otherwise provided for, and which shall be established by Law: but the Congress may by Law vest the Appointment of such inferior Officers, as they think proper, in the President alone, in the Courts of Law, or in the Heads of Departments.

The President shall have Power to fill up all Vacancies that may happen during the Recess of the Senate, by granting Commissions which shall expire at the End of their next Session.

Section 3 - State of the Union, Convening Congress

He shall from time to time give to the Congress Information of the State of the Union, and recommend to their Consideration such Measures as he shall judge necessary and expedient; he may, on extraordinary Occasions, convene both Houses, or either of them, and in Case of Disagreement between them, with Respect to the Time of Adjournment, may adjourn them to such Time as he shall think proper; he shall receive Ambassadors and other public Ministers; he shall take Care that the Laws be faithfully executed, and shall Commission all the Officers of the United States.

Section 4 - Disqualification

The President, Vice President and all civil Officers of the United States, shall be removed from Office on Impeachment for, and Conviction of, Treason, Bribery, or other high Crimes and Misdemeanors.

Article III. - The Judicial Branch

Section 1 - Judicial powers

The judicial Power of the United States, shall be vested in one Supreme Court, and in such inferior Courts as the Congress may from time to time ordain and establish. The Judges, both of the supreme and inferior Courts, shall hold their Offices during good Behavior, and shall, at stated Times, receive for their Services a Compensation which shall not be diminished during their Continuance in Office.

Section 2 - Trial by Jury, Original Jurisdiction, Jury Trials

(The judicial Power shall extend to all Cases, in Law and Equity, arising under this Constitution, the Laws of the United States, and Treaties made, or which shall be made, under their Authority; to all Cases affecting Ambassadors, other public Ministers and Consuls; to all Cases of admiralty and maritime Jurisdiction; *to Controversies to which the United States shall be a Party; to Controversies between two or more States; between a State and Citizens of another State; between Citizens of different States; between Citizens of the same State claiming Lands under Grants of different States, and between a State, or the Citizens thereof, and foreign States, Citizens or Subjects.)* **(This section in parentheses is modified by the 11th Amendment.)**

In all Cases affecting Ambassadors, other public Ministers and Consuls, and those in which a State shall be Party, the Supreme Court shall have original Jurisdiction. In all the other Cases before mentioned, the Supreme Court shall have appellate Jurisdiction, both as to Law and Fact, with such Exceptions, and under such Regulations as the Congress shall make.

The Trial of all Crimes, except in Cases of Impeachment, shall be by Jury; and such Trial shall be held in the State where the said Crimes shall have been committed; but when not committed within any State, the Trial shall be at such Place or Places as the Congress may by Law have directed.

Section 3 - Treason

Treason against the United States shall consist only in levying War against them, or in adhering to their Enemies, giving them Aid and Comfort. No Person shall be convicted of Treason unless on the Testimony of two Witnesses to the same overt Act, or on Confession in open Court.

The Congress shall have power to declare the Punishment of Treason, but no Attainder of Treason shall work Corruption of Blood, or Forfeiture except during the Life of the Person attainted.

Article. IV. - The States

Section 1 - Each State to Honor all others

Full Faith and Credit shall be given in each State to the public Acts, Records, and judicial Proceedings of every other State. And the Congress may by general Laws prescribe the Manner in which such Acts, Records and Proceedings shall be proved, and the Effect thereof.

Section 2 - State citizens, Extradition

The Citizens of each State shall be entitled to all Privileges and Immunities of Citizens in the several States.

A Person charged in any State with Treason, Felony, or other Crime, who shall flee from Justice, and be found in another State, shall on demand of the executive Authority of the State from which he fled, be delivered up, to be removed to the State having Jurisdiction of the Crime.

(No Person held to Service or Labour in one State, under the Laws thereof, escaping into another, shall, in Consequence of any Law or Regulation therein, be discharged from such Service or Labour, But shall be delivered up on Claim of the Party to whom such Service or *Labour may be due.)* **(This clause in parentheses is superseded by the 13th Amendment.)**

Section 3 - New States

New States may be admitted by the Congress into this Union; but no new States shall be formed or erected within the Jurisdiction of any other State; nor any State be formed by the Junction of two or more States, or parts of States, without the Consent of the Legislatures of the States concerned as well as of the Congress.

The Congress shall have Power to dispose of and make all needful Rules and Regulations respecting the Territory or other Property belonging to the United States; and nothing in this Constitution shall be so construed as to Prejudice any Claims of the United States, or of any particular State.

Section 4 - Republican government

The United States shall guarantee to every State in this Union a Republican Form of Government, and shall protect each of them against Invasion; and on Application of the Legislature, or of the Executive (when the Legislature cannot be convened) against domestic Violence.

Article. V. - Amendment

The Congress, whenever two thirds of both Houses shall deem it necessary, shall propose Amendments to this Constitution, or, on the Application of the Legislatures of two thirds of the several States, shall call a Convention for proposing Amendments, which, in either Case, shall be valid to all Intents and Purposes, as part of this Constitution, when ratified by the Legislatures of three fourths of the several States, or by Conventions in three fourths thereof, as the one or the other Mode of Ratification may be proposed by the Congress; Provided that no Amendment which may be made prior to the Year One thousand eight hundred and eight shall in any Manner affect the first and fourth Clauses in the Ninth Section of the first Article; and that no State, without its Consent, shall be deprived of its equal Suffrage in the Senate.

Article. VI. - Debts, Supremacy, Oaths

All Debts contracted and Engagements entered into, before the Adoption of this Constitution, shall be as valid against the United States under this Constitution, as under the Confederation.

This Constitution, and the Laws of the United States which shall be made in Pursuance thereof; and all Treaties made, or which shall be made, under the Authority of the United States, shall be the supreme Law of the Land; and the Judges in every State shall be bound thereby, any Thing in the Constitution or Laws of any State to the Contrary notwithstanding.

The Senators and Representatives before mentioned, and the Members of the several State Legislatures, and all executive and judicial Officers, both of the United States and of the several States, shall be bound by Oath or Affirmation, to support this Constitution; but no religious Test shall ever be required as a Qualification to any Office or public Trust under the United States.

Article. VII. - Ratification Documents

The Ratification of the Conventions of nine States shall be sufficient for the Establishment of this Constitution between the States so ratifying the same.

Done in Convention by the Unanimous Consent of the States present the Seventeenth Day of September in the Year of our Lord one thousand seven hundred and Eighty seven and of the Independence of the United States of America the Twelfth. In Witness whereof We have hereunto subscribed our Names.

Go Washington - President and deputy from Virginia

New Hampshire - John Langdon, Nicholas Gilman
Massachusetts - Nathaniel Gorham, Rufus King

Connecticut - Wm Saml Johnson, Roger Sherman

New York - Alexander Hamilton

New Jersey - Wil Livingston, David Brearley, Wm Paterson, Jona. Dayton

Pensylvania - B Franklin, Thomas Mifflin, Robt Morris, Geo. Clymer, Thos FitzSimons, Jared Ingersoll, James Wilson, Gouv Morris

Delaware - Geo. Read, Gunning Bedford jun, John Dickinson, Richard Bassett, Jaco. Broom

Maryland - James McHenry, Dan of St Tho Jenifer, Danl Carroll

Virginia - John Blair, James Madison Jr.

North Carolina - Wm Blount, Richd Dobbs Spaight, Hu Williamson

South Carolina - J. Rutledge, Charles Cotesworth Pinckney, Charles Pinckney, Pierce Butler

Georgia - William Few, Abr Baldwin

Attest: William Jackson, Secretary

CHAPTER ELEVEN
The Amendments

The following are the Amendments to the Constitution. The first ten Amendments collectively are commonly known as the Bill of Rights.

Amendment 1 - Freedom of Religion, Press, Expression. Ratified 12/15/1791.

Congress shall make no law respecting an establishment of religion, or prohibiting the free exercise thereof; or abridging the freedom of speech, or of the press; or the right of the people peaceably to assemble, and to petition the Government for a redress of grievances.

Amendment 2 - Right to Bear Arms. Ratified 12/15/1791.

A well regulated Militia, being necessary to the security of a free State, the right of the people to keep and bear Arms, shall not be infringed.

Amendment 3 - Quartering of Soldiers. Ratified 12/15/1791.

No Soldier shall, in time of peace be quartered in any house, without the consent of the Owner, nor in time of war, but in a manner to be prescribed by law.

Amendment 4 - Search and Seizure. Ratified 12/15/1791.

The right of the people to be secure in their persons, houses, papers, and effects, against unreasonable searches and seizures, shall not be violated, and no Warrants shall issue, but upon probable cause, supported by Oath or affirmation, and particularly describing the place to be searched, and the persons or things to be seized.

Amendment 5 - Trial and Punishment, Compensation for Takings. Ratified 12/15/1791.

No person shall be held to answer for a capital, or otherwise infamous crime, unless on a presentment or indictment of a Grand Jury, except in cases arising in the land or naval forces, or in the Militia, when in actual service in time of War or public danger; nor shall any person be subject for the same offense to be twice put in jeopardy of life or limb; nor shall be compelled in any criminal case to be a witness against himself, nor be deprived of life, liberty, or property, without due process of law; nor shall private property be taken for public use, without just compensation.

Amendment 6 - Right to Speedy Trial, Confrontation of Witnesses. Ratified 12/15/1791.

In all criminal prosecutions, the accused shall enjoy the right to a speedy and public trial, by an impartial jury of the State and district wherein the crime shall have been committed, which district shall have been previously ascertained by law, and to be informed of the nature and cause of the accusation; to be confronted with the witnesses against him; to have compulsory process for obtaining witnesses in his favor, and to have the Assistance of Counsel for his defense.

Amendment 7 - Trial by Jury in Civil Cases. Ratified 12/15/1791.

In Suits at common law, where the value in controversy shall exceed twenty dollars, the right of trial by jury shall be preserved, and no fact tried by a jury, shall be otherwise re-examined in any Court of the United States, than according to the rules of the common law.

Amendment 8 - Cruel and Unusual Punishment. Ratified 12/15/1791.

Excessive bail shall not be required, nor excessive fines imposed, nor cruel and unusual punishments inflicted.

Amendment 9 - Construction of Constitution. Ratified 12/15/1791.

The enumeration in the Constitution, of certain rights, shall not be construed to deny or disparage others retained by the people.

Amendment 10 - Powers of the States and People. Ratified 12/15/1791.

The powers not delegated to the United States by the Constitution, nor prohibited by it to the States, are reserved to the States respectively, or to the people.

Amendment 11 - Judicial Limits. Ratified 2/7/1795.

The Judicial power of the United States shall not be construed to extend to any suit in law or equity, commenced or prosecuted against one of the United States by Citizens of another State, or by Citizens or Subjects of any Foreign State.

Amendment 12 - Choosing the President, Vice-President. Ratified 6/15/1804.

The Electoral College

The Electors shall meet in their respective states, and vote by ballot for President and Vice-President, one of whom, at least, shall not be an inhabitant of the same state with themselves; they shall name in their ballots the person voted for as President, and in distinct ballots the person voted for as Vice-President, and they shall make distinct lists of all persons voted for as President, and of all persons voted for as Vice-President and of the number of votes for each, which lists they shall sign and certify, and transmit sealed to the seat of the government of the United States, directed to the President of the Senate;

The President of the Senate shall, in the presence of the Senate and House of Representatives, open all the certificates and the votes shall then be counted;

The person having the greatest Number of votes for President, shall be the President, if such number be a majority of the whole number of Electors appointed; and if no person have such majority, then from the persons having the highest numbers not exceeding three on the list of those voted for as President, the House of Representatives shall choose immediately, by ballot, the President. But in choosing the President, the votes shall be taken by states, the representation from each state having one vote; a quorum for this purpose shall consist of a member or members from two-thirds of the states, and a majority of all the states shall be necessary to a choice. And if the House of Representatives shall not choose a President whenever the right of choice shall devolve upon them, before the fourth day of March next following, then the Vice-President shall act as President, as in the case of the death or other constitutional disability of the President.

The person having the greatest number of votes as Vice-President, shall be the Vice-President, if such number be a majority of the whole number of Electors appointed, and if no person have a majority, then from the two highest numbers on the list, the Senate shall choose the Vice-President; a quorum for the purpose shall consist of two-thirds of the whole number of Senators, and a majority of the whole number shall be necessary to a choice. But no person constitutionally ineligible to the office of President shall be eligible to that of Vice-President of the United States.

Amendment 13 - Slavery Abolished. Ratified 12/6/1865.

1. Neither slavery nor involuntary servitude, except as a punishment for crime whereof the party shall have been duly convicted, shall exist within the United States, or any place subject to their jurisdiction.

2. Congress shall have power to enforce this article by appropriate legislation.

Amendment 14 - Citizenship Rights. Ratified 7/9/1868.

1. All persons born or naturalized in the United States, and subject to the jurisdiction thereof, are citizens of the United States and of the State wherein they reside. No State shall make or enforce any law which shall abridge the privileges or immunities of citizens of the United States; nor shall any State deprive any person of life, liberty, or property, without due process of law; nor deny to any person within its jurisdiction the equal protection of the laws.

2. Representatives shall be apportioned among the several States according to their respective numbers, counting the whole number of persons in each State, excluding Indians not taxed. But when the right to vote at any election for the choice of electors for President and Vice-President of the United States, Representatives in Congress, the Executive and Judicial officers of a State, or the members of the Legislature thereof, is denied to any of the male inhabitants of such State, being twenty-one years of age, and citizens of the United States, or in any way abridged, except for participation in rebellion, or other crime, the basis of representation therein shall be reduced in the proportion which the number of such male citizens shall bear to the whole number of male citizens twenty-one years of age in such State.

3. No person shall be a Senator or Representative in Congress, or elector of President and Vice-President, or hold any office, civil or military, under the United States, or under any State, who, having previously taken an oath, as a member of Congress, or as an officer of the United States, or as a member of any State legislature, or as an executive or judicial officer of any State, to support the Constitution of the United States, shall have engaged in insurrection or rebellion against the same, or given aid or comfort to the enemies thereof. But Congress may by a vote of two-thirds of each House, remove such disability.

4. The validity of the public debt of the United States, authorized by law, including debts incurred

for payment of pensions and bounties for services in suppressing insurrection or rebellion, shall not be questioned. But neither the United States nor any State shall assume or pay any debt or obligation incurred in aid of insurrection or rebellion against the United States, or any claim for the loss or emancipation of any slave; but all such debts, obligations and claims shall be held illegal and void.

5. The Congress shall have power to enforce, by appropriate legislation, the provisions of this article.

Amendment 15 - Race No Bar to Vote. Ratified 2/3/1870.

1. The right of citizens of the United States to vote shall not be denied or abridged by the United States or by any State on account of race, color, or previous condition of servitude.

2. The Congress shall have power to enforce this article by appropriate legislation.

Amendment 16 - Status of Income Tax Clarified. Ratified 2/3/1913.

The Congress shall have power to lay and collect taxes on incomes, from whatever source derived, without apportionment among the several States, and without regard to any census or enumeration.

Amendment 17 - Senators Elected by Popular Vote. Ratified 4/8/1913.

The Senate of the United States shall be composed of two Senators from each State, elected by the people thereof, for six years; and each Senator shall have one vote. The electors in each State shall have the qualifications requisite for electors of the most numerous branch of the State legislatures.

When vacancies happen in the representation of any State in the Senate, the executive authority of such State shall issue writs of election to fill such vacancies: Provided, that the legislature of any State may empower the executive thereof to make temporary appointments until the people fill the vacancies by election as the legislature may direct.

This amendment shall not be so construed as to affect the election or term of any Senator chosen before it becomes valid as part of the Constitution.

Amendment 18 - Liquor Abolished. Ratified 1/16/1919. Repealed by Amendment 21, 12/5/1933.

1. After one year from the ratification of this article the manufacture, sale, or transportation of intoxicating liquors within, the importation thereof into, or the exportation thereof from the United States and all territory subject to the jurisdiction thereof for beverage purposes is hereby prohibited.

2. The Congress and the several States shall have concurrent power to enforce this article by appropriate legislation.

3. This article shall be inoperative unless it shall have been ratified as an amendment to the Constitution by the legislatures of the several States, as provided in the Constitution, within seven years from the date of the submission hereof to the States by the Congress.

Amendment 19 - Women's Suffrage. Ratified 8/18/1920.

The right of citizens of the United States to vote shall not be denied or abridged by the United States or by any State on account of sex.

Congress shall have power to enforce this article by appropriate legislation.

Amendment 20 - Presidential, Congressional Terms. Ratified 1/23/1933.

1. The terms of the President and Vice President shall end at noon on the 20th day of January, and the terms of Senators and Representatives at noon on the 3d day of January, of the years in which such terms would have ended if this article had not been ratified; and the terms of their successors shall then begin.

2. The Congress shall assemble at least once in every year, and such meeting shall begin at noon on

the 3d day of January, unless they shall by law appoint a different day.

3. If, at the time fixed for the beginning of the term of the President, the President elect shall have died, the Vice President elect shall become President. If a President shall not have been chosen before the time fixed for the beginning of his term, or if the President elect shall have failed to qualify, then the Vice President elect shall act as President until a President shall have qualified; and the Congress may by law provide for the case wherein neither a President elect nor a Vice President elect shall have qualified, declaring who shall then act as President, or the manner in which one who is to act shall be selected, and such person shall act accordingly until a President or Vice President shall have qualified.

4. The Congress may by law provide for the case of the death of any of the persons from whom the House of Representatives may choose a President whenever the right of choice shall have devolved upon them, and for the case of the death of any of the persons from whom the Senate may choose a Vice President whenever the right of choice shall have devolved upon them.

5. Sections 1 and 2 shall take effect on the 15th day of October following the ratification of this article.

6. This article shall be inoperative unless it shall have been ratified as an amendment to the Constitution by the legislatures of three-fourths of the

several States within seven years from the date of its submission.

Amendment 21 - Amendment 18 Repealed. Ratified 12/5/1933.

1. The eighteenth article of amendment to the Constitution of the United States is hereby repealed.

2. The transportation or importation into any State, Territory, or possession of the United States for delivery or use therein of intoxicating liquors, in violation of the laws thereof, is hereby prohibited.

3. The article shall be inoperative unless it shall have been ratified as an amendment to the Constitution by conventions in the several States, as provided in the Constitution, within seven years from the date of the submission hereof to the States by the Congress.

Amendment 22 - Presidential Term Limits. Ratified 2/27/1951.

1. No person shall be elected to the office of the President more than twice, and no person who has held the office of President, or acted as President, for more than two years of a term to which some other person was elected President shall be elected to the office of the President more than once. But this Article shall not apply to any person holding the office of President, when this Article was proposed by the Congress, and shall not prevent any person who may be holding the office of President, or act-

ing as President, during the term within which this Article becomes operative from holding the office of President or acting as President during the remainder of such term.

2. This article shall be inoperative unless it shall have been ratified as an amendment to the Constitution by the legislatures of three-fourths of the several States within seven years from the date of its submission to the States by the Congress.

Amendment 23 - Presidential Vote for District of Columbia. Ratified 3/29/1961.

1. The District constituting the seat of Government of the United States shall appoint in such manner as the Congress may direct: A number of electors of President and Vice President equal to the whole number of Senators and Representatives in Congress to which the District would be entitled if it were a State, but in no event more than the least populous State; they shall be in addition to those appointed by the States, but they shall be considered, for the purposes of the election of President and Vice President, to be electors appointed by a State; and they shall meet in the District and perform such duties as provided by the twelfth article of amendment.

2. The Congress shall have power to enforce this article by appropriate legislation.

Amendment 24 - Poll Tax Barred. Ratified 1/23/1964.

1. The right of citizens of the United States to vote in any primary or other election for President or Vice President, for electors for President or Vice President, or for Senator or Representative in Congress, shall not be denied or abridged by the United States or any State by reason of failure to pay any poll tax or other tax.

2. The Congress shall have power to enforce this article by appropriate legislation.

Amendment 25 - Presidential Disability and Succession. Ratified 2/10/1967.

1. In case of the removal of the President from office or of his death or resignation, the Vice President shall become President.

2. Whenever there is a vacancy in the office of the Vice President, the President shall nominate a Vice President who shall take office upon confirmation by a majority vote of both Houses of Congress.

3. Whenever the President transmits to the President pro tempore of the Senate and the Speaker of the House of Representatives his written declaration that he is unable to discharge the powers and duties of his office, and until he transmits to them a written declaration to the contrary, such powers and duties shall be discharged by the Vice President as Acting President.

4. Whenever the Vice President and a majority of either the principal officers of the executive departments or of such other body as Congress may by law provide, transmit to the President pro tempore of the Senate and the Speaker of the House of Representatives their written declaration that the President is unable to discharge the powers and duties of his office, the Vice President shall immediately assume the powers and duties of the office as Acting President.

Thereafter, when the President transmits to the President pro tempore of the Senate and the Speaker of the House of Representatives his written declaration that no inability exists, he shall resume the powers and duties of his office unless the Vice President and a majority of either the principal officers of the executive department or of such other body as Congress may by law provide, transmit within four days to the President pro tempore of the Senate and the Speaker of the House of Representatives their written declaration that the President is unable to discharge the powers and duties of his office. Thereupon Congress shall decide the issue, assembling within forty eight hours for that purpose if not in session. If the Congress, within twenty one days after receipt of the latter written declaration, or, if Congress is not in session, within twenty one days after Congress is required to assemble, determines by two thirds vote of both Houses that the President is unable to discharge the powers and duties of his office, the Vice President shall continue to discharge the same as Acting President;

otherwise, the President shall resume the powers and duties of his office.

Amendment 26 - Voting Age Set to 18 Years. Ratified 7/1/1971.

1. The right of citizens of the United States, who are eighteen years of age or older, to vote shall not be denied or abridged by the United States or by any State on account of age.

2. The Congress shall have power to enforce this article by appropriate legislation.

Amendment 27 - Limiting Congressional Pay Increases. Ratified 5/7/1992.

No law, varying the compensation for the services of the Senators and Representatives, shall take effect, until an election of Representatives shall have intervened.

CHAPTER TWELVE
U.S. Political Parties

The following is a list of the names and web sites of political parties other than the three mentioned in earlier chapters.

Green Party (41)
www.gp.org

Reform Party (11)
www.reformparty.org
Constitution Party (17)
 www.constitutionparty.org

Communist Party USA (3)
www.cpusa.org

Workers World Party
Working-class party that fights against capitalism.
www.workers.org

Natural Law Party (3)
www.natural-law.org
Socialist Party USA (6)
www.votesocialist.org

New Part
www.newparty.org

Socialist Labor Party of America (2)
www.slp.org

Timesizing Party of Massachusetts
Platform is based on upsizing markets by downsizing the workweek, not the workforce.
www.timesizing.com

Freedom Socialist Party
Revolutionary feminist organization dedicated to the replacement of capitalist rule by a genuine workers' democracy.
www.socialism.com

American Reform Party
Free-standing, national group that in 1997 formally split from Ross Perot and his

Dallas-based Reform Party.
www.americanreform.org

United States Independent American Party
United by a common Religious Right ideology.
www.usiap.org

Pirate Party of the United States
Political party dedicated to the reform of copyright and the patent system, with a focus on an individual's right to privacy.
www.pirate-party.us

America First Party
Site includes mission statement and party platform.
ww.americafirstparty.org

Young Democratic Socialists

Youth section of the Democratic Socialists of America.

www.ydsusa.org

Constitutionalist Party

New political party dedicated to the advancement of human liberty and adherence to the U.S. Constitution.

home.earthlink.net/~jmarkels/cp.html

Pot Party 2002

Movement to legalize marijuana, implement proportional representation, and mandate pot growing.

www.pot-party.com

Workers Party USA

www.workersparty.org

Christian Falangist Party of America

Official site of the CFPA, a political party that was founded in Philadelphia in 1985. The Christian Falangists' beliefs are right-wing, between Conservatives and Fascists on the political spectrum.

www.falangist.com

America's Party

A new party for Americans wanting responsive government.

www.americasparty.org

Southern Party (3)

www.southernparty2000.org

American Conservative Party (1)

www.njconservativeparty.org

Jeffersonian Party

Includes the mission and platform of the party.
www.jeffersonianparty.com

New American Independent Party

Alternative grassroots political party that promotes
sustainable policies and helps members join ballot
access groups. Website provides information about
various issues supported by the party.
www.newamericanindependent.com

Christian Alliance

US-based Christian political party.
www.christianalliance.com

CHAPTER THIRTEEN
Voting Instructions and Forms

"We hang the petty thieves and appoint the great ones to public office."

Aesop

- Frequently Asked Questions
- Questions about Voter Registration
- Questions about Voting
- Questions about Ballot Measures

QUESTIONS ABOUT VOTER REGISTRATION

Question: Who can register to vote?

Answer: In order to register to vote, a person must:
(Varies somewhat by state)

- Be a citizen of the United States
- Be a resident of your State
- Be at least 18 years of age as of the day of the next election; Not be in prison or on parole for the conviction of a felony; and not be deemed by an appropriate court to be mentally incompetent.

Question: How do I register to vote?

Answer: To register to vote you must obtain and complete voter registration form. Voter registration forms can be obtained by:

Caring your local county elections official and requesting a form filling out a voter registration card on-line (a pre-typed registration form will then be mailed to you); or downloading a voter registration form from your states web site and mailing it to your county elections official.

Question: What is the deadline to register to vote?

Answer: The deadline to register to vote is 15 days prior to each local and state-wide Election Day.

Question: I have just moved. Should I re-register?

Answer: Yes, your voter registration should always reflect your current residence address.

Question: I did not vote in the last election. Do I need to re-register?

Answer: In general, you are registered for as long as you remain at the same address, and you should continue to receive election materials in the mail. However, if you have not voted in the last several elections, you may be sent a request to confirm that you have not moved, and your registration may be eventually canceled.

Question: Do I have to be registered to vote in order to register other voters?

No, you do not need to be a registered voter in order to register voters. There are no statutory restrictions on who can register people to vote.

Question: Can an ex-felon register to vote and vote?

Answer: An ex-felon can register to vote and vote if he/she is not in prison or on parole for a felony conviction.

Question: I sent in my voter registration from a month ago and I still don't know where to vote. Did you receive my registration card?

Answer: The form should be pre-addressed already. Generally, it goes to your county elections official, but if it is a statewide (i.e. not specific to one county) form, it may come to the Secretary of State to be forwarded to the appropriate county elections office.

You may find the address for your county elections office by clicking on "Who Is My County Elections Official?"

Question: Do I have to be deputized to register people to vote?

Answer: No, you do not have to be deputized to register people to vote.

Question: How many voter registration affidavits can I get if I want to register people in my community?

Answer: There is no limit to the number of voter registration affidavits a person may obtain. However, the Secretary of State does not require the requester to complete a Voter Registration Card Statement of Distribution Form.

Question: How can a person prove his or her citizen-ship?

Answer: A person may prove he or she is a citizen by his or her certification under penalty of perjury on the affidavit of registration (for voter registration purposes only)."

Question: Why is the Department of Motor Vehicles involved in voter registration?

Answer: The National Voter Registration Act of 1993 (also known as Motor Voter) permits persons conducting business at a DMV office to register to vote or update their voter registration information.

CHAPTER FOURTEEN
Questions About Voting

Question: How can I vote a Vote-By-Mail ballot?

Answer: Any registered voter may vote by a "vote-by-mail" ballot. You may vote a vote-by-mail ballot by:

Applying in writing to your county elections official; or completing the vote-by-mail ballot application that is included in your Sample Ballot, which your county elections official will mail to you prior to each election; or downloading and completing a vote-by-mail ballot application from our web site.

Question: When may I apply for a vote-by-mail ballot?

Answer: Elections officials process applications 29 days to 7 days before an election. You may request a vote-by-mail ballot more than 29 days before an election, but not fewer than 7 days in advance.

Question: When is the last day to return my voted vote-by-mail ballot?

Answer: Vote-by-mail ballot must be received by the elections official no later than the close of polls (8 p.m.) on Election Day.

Question: How do I turn in my vote-by-mail ballot on Election Day?

Answer: You may return it in person to any polling place in your county or to the county elections office on Election Day. If, because of illness or physical disability, you are unable to return the ballot yourself, you may designate a spouse, child, parent, grand-parent, sibling, or a person residing in the same house hold to return the ballot to the elections official or the precinct board at any polling place within the jurisdiction. The ballot must be received by the elections official or the precinct board before the close the polls (8 p.m.) on Election Day in order to be counted.

Question: Where is my polling place?

Answer: Your polling place location will be printed on the Sample Ballot you receive from your local county elections official prior to an election. You may also contact your local county elections office for polling place information. Approximately on month prior to all primary an general elections, the Secretary of

State's office will have a polling place lookup feature on this web site.

Question: What hours are polling place locations open?

Answer: All polling place locations are open on the day of an election from 7:00am until 8:00pm.

Question: How do I find out what my legislative and congressional districts are?

Answer: You may contact your county elections official.

Question: Why was my precinct/polling place changed?

Answer: Counties try to use the same polling place for each countywide election so your polling place normally does not change between the primary and the general election. If the county is conducting smaller local elections – where the turnout will be lower – the county may not need as many polling places so it may consolidate precincts into fewer polling places. In this case, your "usual" polling place could change – sometimes across town. This can be confusing. You can always determine where your polling places by looking at the back of your sample ballot, which you will receive from your county elections office. The back cover contains the name and address of your polling place. You can also call your county elections office, and they will tell you where your polling place is located.

You also have the option of applying, to your county elections office for permanent vote-by-mail voter status. For each election in which you are eligible to vote your county elections office will automatically send you the appropriate ballot. All you will need to do is vote, provide the required information, and return the voted ballot to your county elections office by close of the polls (8:00 p.m.) on Election Day.

Question: Why am I in a mail ballot (vote-by-mail) precinct?

Answer: State election law provides that precincts with fewer than 250 voters may be sent vote-by-mail ballots instead of setting up a polling place. Upon receiving a vote-by-mail ballot, all you need to do is vote for the contests on the ballot, provide the required information, and mail the voted ballot back to your county elections office. It must be received in your county elections office by the close of the polls (8:00 p.m.) on Election Day.

If you cannot mail your voted vote-by-mail ballot to your county elections office, you can cast your voted ballot at any polling place in your county by the close of the polls (8:00 p.m.) on Election Day. To determine the location of a nearby polling place, you can contact your county elections office. By clicking on the following link, you can find county contact information County Elections Officials.

Question: Is there a toll-free telephone number I can call regarding voter information?

Answer: Yes. The Secretary of State has established a toll free hotline for requests for voter registration forms and to report suspicions of voting or registration irregularities. Check with your state office for the number.

Question: Are election returns for state offices on the Internet somewhere?

Answer: We have put the election results from past statewide elections on our web site.

Question: What can be done to increase voter participation?

Answer: The Secretary of State's office has been working with youth organizations, community partners and minority organizations to increase voter anticipation. We are always looking for better ways to reach out and engage citizens in the voting process.

Please look at our Voter Education web page to learn about some of the programs and events your state may be currently working on.

QUESTIONS ABOUT BALLOT MEASURES

Question: When are numbers assigned to Propositions?

Answer: Contact your state for an "Initiative Guide Handbook."

Question: How many signatures does it take to qualify a state wide initiative?

Answer: The number of signatures required for initiative statutes must be equal to at least 5% of the total votes cast for Governor at the last gubernatorial election. The number of signatures required for initiative constitutional amendments must be equal to at least 8% of the total votes cast for Governor at the last gubernatorial election. Varies by state.

Question: When is the deadline for initiatives to qualify for the ballet?

Answer: Measures have to qualify by 131 days before election, thereby allowing adequate time to produce the ballot pamphlet and air both sides of the issues. (May vary by state.)

Free to Vote   Able to Vote   Ready to Vote

STEPS TO <u>AVOID</u> WHEN MARKING YOUR BALLOT

Vote-by-Mail Ballot:
How to make sure your ballot counts!

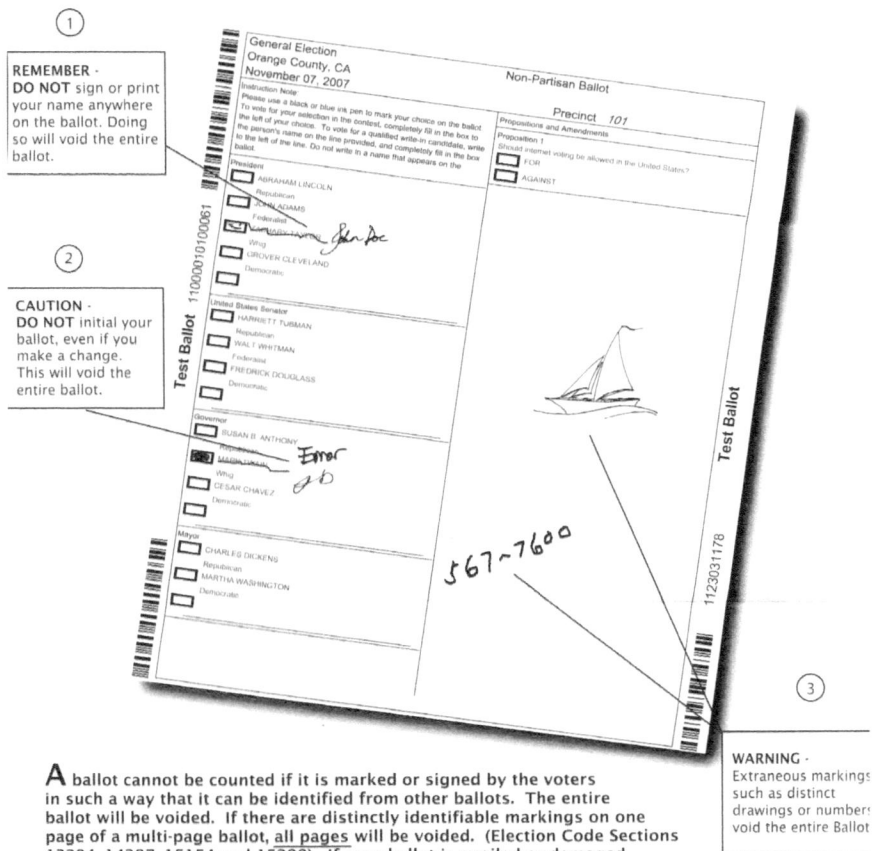

① REMEMBER · **DO NOT** sign or print your name anywhere on the ballot. Doing so will void the entire ballot.

② CAUTION · **DO NOT** initial your ballot, even if you make a change. This will void the entire ballot.

③ WARNING · Extraneous markings such as distinct drawings or numbers void the entire Ballot

A ballot cannot be counted if it is marked or signed by the voters in such a way that it can be identified from other ballots. The entire ballot will be voided. If there are distinctly identifiable markings on one page of a multi-page ballot, <u>all pages</u> will be voided. (Election Code Sections 13204, 14287, 15154 and 15208). If your ballot is spoiled or damaged, please call us at (714) 567-7600 for instructions to obtain a second ballot.

FOR MORE INFORMATION, VISIT OUR WEBSITE AT WWW.OCVOTE.COM

ORANGE COUNTY REGISTRAR OF VOTERS 1300 South Grand Avenue Building C Santa Ana 92705 714.567.7600

IMPORTANT!
INSTRUCTIONS FOR COMPLETING YOUR VOTE-BY-MAIL BALLOT

SAMPLE BALLOT PAMPHLETS ARE MAILED 40 DAYS THROUGH 10 DAYS PRIOR TO THE ELECTION AND CAN BE FOUND AT WWW.OCVOTE.COM

HOW TO VOTE YOUR BALLOT: Use a black or blue pen • Completely fill in the entire voting rectangle to the left of the candidate's name or to the left of the word "YES" or "NO" for a measure • **Your ballot will remain secret/Do not sign or place your initials on your ballot. California law prohibits identifying marks on a ballot and any such marks will cause your ballot to be voided.** • To vote for a qualified write-in candidate, write the person's name on the line provided, and completely fill in the voting rectangle to the left of the line • **Do not write in a name that is already printed on the ballot** • If you desire to vote at your polling place, you must surrender your **unvoted** vote-by-mail ballot at the polls.

ENCLOSED IDENTIFICATION (ID) ENVELOPE: Place your voted ballot, and no one else's, in the ID envelope provided • Sign your name and indicate your residence address on the outside of the ID envelope as it appears on your registration affidavit • If a voter cannot sign his/her name, an "X" witnessed by one person is acceptable. The voter's name must be written near the mark and the witness must sign his/her name as a witness (A power of attorney is not acceptable). A signature stamp may also be used if the voter has previously submitted his/her registration affidavit, in the presence of a county elections official, using the signature stamp to sign the affidavit. If your original ballot is lost, spoiled, damaged or marked in error, call (714) 567-7600 for instructions on obtaining a second ballot.

RETURN YOUR BALLOT: You must return your ballot in the ID envelope • You may return your ballot by mail, or in person to the Registrar of Voters office or any polling place in Orange County • Your ballot must be received by the Registrar of Voters office (**postmarks do not count**) or the polling place by 8:00 p.m. on Election Day • If you are ill or disabled, you may designate a spouse, child, parent, grandparent, grandchild, brother, sister, or a person residing in your house to return the ballot for you • The designee must print his/her name, sign, and indicate the relationship to you on the ID envelope.

TOP FIVE REASONS FOR YOUR VOTE-BY-MAIL BALLOT NOT TO BE COUNTED:

1. **No Signature:** You did not sign the ID envelope where indicated.
2. **Late Return:** Your vote-by-mail ballot arrived after 8:00 p.m. on Election Day.
3. **Unnecessary Marks:** You signed, initialed, or placed extraneous marks on your ballot.
4. **Unauthorized Envelope:** Ballot is returned in a different envelope. You **DID NOT** use the ID envelope provided.
5. **Unauthorized Return:** You are unable to return your ballot and **DID NOT** authorize a relative or person residing in your home to return it for you.

Telecommunications Device for the Deaf (714) 567-7008 • www.ocvote.com

ORANGE COUNTY REGISTRAR OF VOTERS | 1300 South Grand Avenue | Building C | Santa Ana 92705 | 714.567.7600

The eSlate Voting System
With <u>The Voter Verifiable Paper Audit Trail</u>

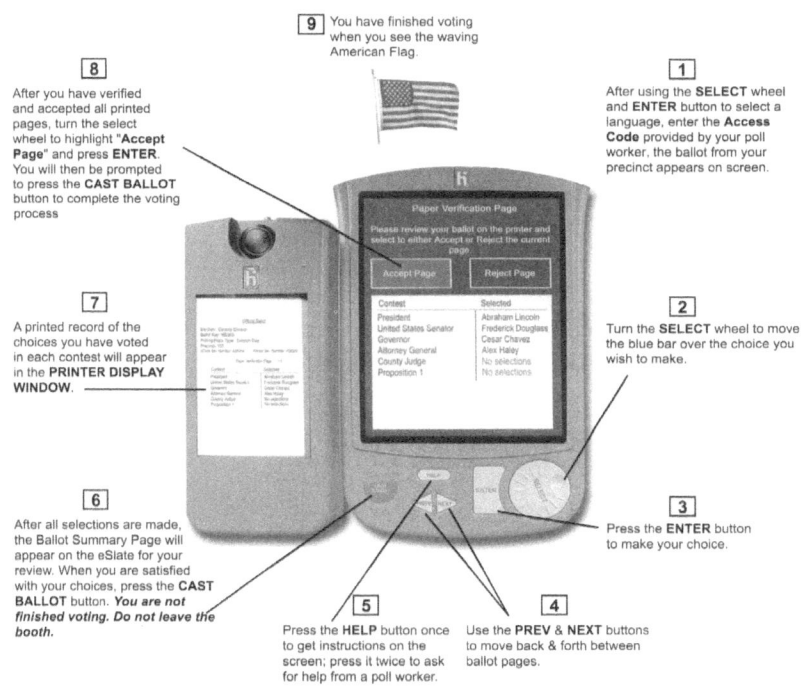

9 You have finished voting when you see the waving American Flag.

8
After you have verified and accepted all printed pages, turn the select wheel to highlight "**Accept Page**" and press **ENTER**. You will then be prompted to press the **CAST BALLOT** button to complete the voting process

1
After using the **SELECT** wheel and **ENTER** button to select a language, enter the **Access Code** provided by your poll worker, the ballot from your precinct appears on screen.

7
A printed record of the choices you have voted in each contest will appear in the **PRINTER DISPLAY WINDOW**.

2
Turn the **SELECT** wheel to move the blue bar over the choice you wish to make.

6
After all selections are made, the Ballot Summary Page will appear on the eSlate for your review. When you are satisfied with your choices, press the **CAST BALLOT** button. *You are not finished voting. Do not leave the booth.*

3
Press the **ENTER** button to make your choice.

5 Press the **HELP** button once to get instructions on the screen; press it twice to ask for help from a poll worker.

4 Use the **PREV & NEXT** buttons to move back & forth between ballot pages.

You can also vote-by-mail or use a paper ballot at your poll site.

For more details visit www.ocvote.com/options

ORANGE COUNTY REGISTRAR OF VOTERS | 1300 South Grand Avenue | Building C | Santa Ana 92705 | 714.567.7600

INSTRUCTIONS TO VOTERS

Voting Electronically at the Polls:

To vote for a candidate whose name appears on the ballot, turn the select wheel to move the blue bar to highlight your choice and press the ENTER button. Where two or more candidates for the same office are to be elected, turn the select wheel to move the blue bar to highlight your choice and press the ENTER button after the names of all candidates for the office for whom you desire to vote, not to exceed, however, the number of candidates to be elected.

To vote for a qualified write-in candidate, turn the select wheel to move the blue bar to highlight the blank space provided for that purpose after the names of the other candidates for the same office and press the ENTER button to type the person's name.

To vote on any measure, turn the select wheel to move the blue bar to highlight your choice in the voting square after the word "Yes" or after the word "No" and press the ENTER button.

Voting on a Paper Ballot at the Polls:

To vote for a candidate whose name appears on the ballot, using a black or blue pen provided, **completely fill in** the rectangle to the left of the candidate's name. Where two or more candidates for the same office are to be elected, **completely fill in** the rectangle to the left of the names of all candidates for the office for whom you desire to vote, not to exceed, however, the number of candidates to be elected.

To vote for a qualified write-in candidate, write the person's name in the blank space provided for that purpose after the names of the other candidates for the same office. Be sure to **completely fill in** the corresponding rectangle.

To vote on any measure, **completely fill in** the rectangle to the left of the word "Yes" or to the left of the word "No."

If you incorrectly mark, tear or deface your ballot, return it to a precinct board member and obtain another. All distinguishing marks and erasures are forbidden and make the ballot void.

Vote for only one selection for each contest, unless otherwise indicated.

Once you have finished voting, place your ballot in the secrecy folder provided and return it to a precinct board member, who will deposit your voted ballot into the ballot box.

Example:

FOR GOVERNOR

Vote for One

☐ THOMAS A. EDISON
☐ ALBERT EINSTEIN
☐ HELEN KELLER
■ FLORENCE NIGHTINGALE
☐ BOOKER T. WASHINGTON
☐ _____

OCVOTE.COM

ORANGE COUNTY REGISTRAR OF VOTERS | 1300 South Grand Avenue | Building C | Santa Ana 92705 | 714.567.7600

OR 052-006

General Instructions

Who Can Use this Application

If you are a U.S. citizen who lives or has an address within the United States, you can use the application in this booklet to:

■ Register to vote in your State,

■ Report a change of name to your voter registration office,

■ Report a change of address to your voter registration office, or

■ Register with a political party.

Exceptions

Please do not use this application if you live outside the United States and its territories and have no home (legal) address in this country, *or* if you are in the military stationed away from home. Use the Federal Postcard Application available to you from military bases, American embassies, or consular offices.

New Hampshire town and city clerks will accept this application only as a request for their own absentee voter mail-in registration form.

North Dakota does not have voter registration.

Wyoming law does not permit mail registration.

How to Find Out If You Are Eligible to Register to Vote in Your State

Each State has its own laws about who may register and vote. Check the information under your State in the State Instructions.

Note: All States require that you be a United States citizen by birth or naturalization to register to vote in federal and State elections. Federal law makes it illegal to falsely claim U.S. citizenship to register to vote in any federal, State, or local election.

Also Note: You **cannot** be registered to vote in more than one place at a time.

How to Fill Out this Application

Use both the Application Instructions and State Instructions to guide you in filling out the application.

First, read the Application Instructions. These instructions will give you important information that applies to everyone using this application.

Next, find your State under the State Instructions. Use these instructions to fill out Boxes 6, 7, and 8. Also refer to these instructions for information about voter eligibility and any oath required for Box 9.

When to Register to Vote

Each State has its own deadline for registering to vote. Check the deadline for your State on the last page of booklet.

How to Submit Your Application

Mail your application to the address listed under you State in the State Instructions. Or, deliver the applic in person to your local voter registration office.

The remaining States that accept the national form v accept copies of the application printed from the com image on regular paper stock, signed by the applican and mailed in an envelope with the correct postage.

First Time Voters Who Register by Mail

If you are registering to vote for the first time in you jurisdiction and are mailing this registration applica you may be required to provide proof of identification first time you vote.

Depending on the specific requirements of your State may avoid providing identification at the polls when vote for the first time by mailing a copy of an identifi tion document together with this application. The lis acceptable documents is included in the State Instruc tions.

Do not include original documents with this application.

Please read the accompanying State Instructions to determine the voter identification requirements for your State.

If You Were Given this Application in a State Agency or Public Office

If you have been given this application in a State agency or public office, it is your choice to use the application or not.

If you decide to use this application to register to vote, you can fill it out and leave it with the State agency or public office. The application will be submitted for you. Or, you can take it with you to mail to the address listed under your State in the State Instructions. You also may take it with you to deliver in person to your local voter registration office.

Note: The name and location of the State agenc or public office where you received the application will remain confidential. It will not appear on you application. Also, if you decide not to use this app cation to register to vote, that decision will remain confidential. It will not affect the service you recei from the agency or office.

Revised 1(

119

Application Instructions

Before filling out the body of the form, please answer the questions on the top of the form as to whether you are a U States citizen and whether you will be 18 years old on or before election day. If you answer no to either of these que tions, you may not use this form to register to vote. However, state specific instructions may provide additional info tion on eligibility to register to vote prior to age 18.

Box 1 — Name

Put in this box your full name in this order — Last, First, Middle. Do not use nicknames or initials.

Note: If this application is for a change of name, please tell us in **Box A** *(on the bottom half of the form)* your full name before you changed it.

Box 2 — Home Address

Put in this box your home address (legal address). Do **not** put your mailing address here if it is different from your home address. Do **not** use a post office box or rural route without a box number. Refer to state-specific instructions for rules regarding use of route numbers.

Note: If you were registered before *but* this is the first time you are registering from the address in Box 2, please tell us in **Box B** *(on the bottom half of the form)* the address where you were registered before. Please give us as much of the address as you can remember.

Also Note: If you live in a rural area but do not have a street address, *or* if you have no address, please show where you live using the map in **Box C** *(at the bottom of the form)*.

Box 3 — Mailing Address

If you get your mail at an address that is different from the address in Box 2, put your mailing address in this box.

Note: If you have no address in Box 2, you **must** write in Box 3 an address where you can be reached by mail.

Box 4 — Date of Birth

Put in this box your date of birth in this order — Month, Day, Year. *Be careful not to use today's date!*

Box 5 — Telephone Number

Most States ask for your telephone number in case there are questions about your application. However, you do **not** have to fill in this box.

Box 6 — ID Number

Federal law requires that states collect from each registrant an identification number. You must refer to your state's specific instructions for item 6 regarding information on what number is acceptable for your state. If you have neither a drivers license nor a social security number, please indicate this on the form and a number will be assigned to you by your state.

Box 7 — Choice of Party

In some States, you must register with a party if you want to take part in that party's primary election, caucus, or convention. To find out if your State requires this, see item 7 in the instructions under your State.

If you want to register with a party, print in the box full name of the party of your choice.

If you do **not** want to register with a party, write "no party" or leave the box blank. Do **not** write in the wo "independent" if you mean "no party," because this m be confused with the name of a political party in your State.

Note: If you do not register with a party, you can s vote in general elections and nonpartisan (nonparty) primary elections.

Box 8 — Race or Ethnic Group

A few States ask for your race or ethnic group, in ord administer the Federal Voting Rights Act. To find ou your State asks for this information, see item 8 in the structions under your State. If so, put in Box 8 the cl that best describes you from the list below:

American Indian *or* Alaskan Native

Asian or Pacific Islander

Black, *not of* Hispanic Origin

Hispanic

Multi-racial

White, *not of* Hispanic Origin

Other

Box 9 — Signature

Review the information in item 9 in the instructions u der your State. Before you sign or make your mark, r sure that:

(1) You meet your State's requirements, and

(2) You understand **all** of Box 9.

Finally, sign your **full** name or make your mark, and print today's date in this order — Month, Day, Year.

If the applicant is unable to sign, put in **Box D** the na address, and telephone number (optional) of the perso who helped the applicant.

State Instructions

California

Registration Deadline — 15 days before the election.

6. ID Number When you register to vote, you must provide your California driver's license or California identification card number, if you have one. If you do not have a driver's license or ID card, you must provide the last four digits of your Social Security Number (SSN). If you do not include this information, you will be required to provide identification when you vote.

7. Choice of Party. Please enter the name of the political party with which you wish to register. If you do not wish to register with any party, enter "Decline to State" in the space provided.

California law allows voters who "decline to state" an affiliation with a qualified political party or who affiliate with a nonqualified political party to vote in the primary election of any qualified political party that files a notice with the Secretary of State allowing them to do so. You can call 1-800-345-VOTE or visit www.ss.ca.gov to learn which political parties are allowing nonaffiliated voters to participate in their primary election.

8. Race or Ethnic Group. Leave blank.

9. Signature. To register in California you must:

• be a citizen of the United States
• be a resident of California
• be at least 18 years of age at the time of the next election
• not be imprisoned or on parole for the conviction of a felony
• not currently be judged mentally incompetent by a court of law
Signature is required. If you meet the requirements listed above, please sign and date the registration card in the space provided.

Attention: Proof of Voter Identification

(Pursuant to the Help America Vote Act of 2002)

Voting in person:

• A first-time voter who registers by mail must present to the appropriate state or local election official:
1) a current and valid photo identification; or

2) a current utility bill, bank statement, government check, paycheck, or other government document that shows the name and address of the voter.

Voting by mail:

• A first-time voter who registers by mail must submit a **COPY** of one of the following documents with his or her absentee ballot:
1) current and valid photo identification; **OR**
2) current utility bill, bank statement, government check, paycheck, or other government document that shows the name and address of the voter.

For Those Who Register by Mail:

Persons who register to vote by mail and submit a driver's license number that the state or local election official can match with an existing state identification record will not be required to provide identification when they vote. Additionally, voters will not be required to provide identification when they vote if they are: (i) provided the right to vote otherwise than in person under the Voting Accessibility for the Elderly and Handicapped Act; or (ii) entitled to vote otherwise than in person under any other Federal law.

These identification requirements only apply to elections in which there is a federal office on the ballot. If you do not provide proof of identification, you may cast a provisional ballot.

Mailing address:

Secretary of State
Elections Division
1500 11th Street
Sacramento, CA 95814

> FOR FASTER PROCESSING MAIL THIS NATIONAL VOTER REGISTRATION FORM DIRECTLY TO YOUR LOCAL COUNTY ELECTIONS OFFICIAL.
>
> CLICK HERE FOR THE ADDRESS!

Revised 10/29/2003

121

Voter Registration Application

Before completing this form, review the General, Application, and State specific instructions.

Are you a citizen of the United States of America? ☐ Yes ☐ No Will you be 18 years old on or before election day? ☐ Yes ☐ No If you checked "No" in response to either of these questions, do not complete form. (Please see state-specific instructions for rules regarding eligibility to register prior to age 18.)		This space for office use only.

1   (Circle one) Mr. Mrs. Miss Ms.   Last Name   First Name   Middle Name(s)   (Circle one) Jr Sr II III IV

2   Home Address   Apt. or Lot #   City/Town   State   Zip Code

3   Address Where You Get Your Mail If Different From Above   City/Town   State   Zip Code

4   Date of Birth   /   /   Month Day Year

5   Telephone Number (optional)

6   ID Number - (See Item 6 in the instructions for your state)

7   Choice of Party (see item 7 in the instructions for your State)

8   Race or Ethnic Group (see item 8 in the instructions for your State)

9   I have reviewed my state's instructions and I swear/affirm that:
- I am a United States citizen
- I meet the eligibility requirements of my state and subscribe to any oath required.
- The information I have provided is true to the best of my knowledge under penalty of perjury. If I have provided false information, I may be fined, imprisoned, or (if not a U.S. citizen) deported from or refused entry to the United States.

Please sign full name (or put mark) ▲

Date: /   /   Month Day Year

If you are registering to vote for the first time: please refer to the application instructions for information on submitting copies of valid identification documents with this form.

Please fill out the sections below if they apply to you.

If this application is for a **change of name**, what was your name before you changed it?

A   Mr. Mrs. Miss Ms.   Last Name   First Name   Middle Name(s)   (Circle one) Jr Sr II III IV

If you were **registered before** but this is the first time you are registering from the address in Box 2, what was your address where you were registered before?

B   Street (or route and box number)   Apt. or Lot #   City/Town/County   State   Zip Code

If you live in a rural area but do not have a street number, or if you have no address, please show on the map where you live.

C
- Write in the names of the crossroads (or streets) nearest to where you live.
- Draw an **X** to show where you live.
- Use a dot to show any schools, churches, stores, or other landmarks near where you live, and write the name of the landmark.

NORTH ↑

Example | Route #2 | ● Grocery Store | Woodchuck Road | Public School ● | X

If the applicant is unable to sign, who helped the applicant fill out this application? Give name, address and phone number (phone number optional).

D

Mail this application to the address provided for your State.

Copy Right 2008. All rights reserved ©